Enfolded in Christ

Dear Richard

With thanks for
your example, prayers
and support,

John. Prin

14. 06. 18

Enfolded in Christ

The Inner Life of a Priest

John-Francis Friendship

CANTERBURY
PRESS
Norwich

© John-Francis Friendship 2018

First published in 2018 by the Canterbury Press Norwich
Editorial office
3rd Floor, Invicta House
108–114 Golden Lane
London EC1Y 0TG, UK
www.canterburypress.co.uk

Canterbury Press is an imprint of Hymns Ancient & Modern Ltd
(a registered charity)

Ancient
&Modern

Hymns Ancient & Modern® is a registered trademark of
Hymns Ancient & Modern Ltd
13A Hellesdon Park Road, Norwich,
Norfolk NR6 5DR, UK

Scripture quotations are from the New Revised Standard Version
of the Bible, Anglicized Edition, copyright © 1989, 1995 by
the Division of Christian Education of the National Council
of the Churches of Christ in the USA. Used by permission.
All rights reserved.

British Library Cataloguing in Publication data

A catalogue record for this book is available
from the British Library

978 1 78622 046 2

Typeset by Regent Typesetting
Printed and bound in Great Britain by
CPI Group (UK) Ltd

Contents

APPENDICES

Expanded Contents

For the purposes of navigation, the following expanded contents list includes text headings.

This book is dedicated to the
Sacred and Compassionate
Hearts of
Jesus and Mary,
and to Benedict, Francis and Ignatius
whose lives continue to inspire.

❧

It is no longer I who live,
but it is Christ who lives in me.
And the life I now live in the flesh
I live by faith in the Son of God,
who loved me
and gave himself for me.
(The Letter of St Paul to the Galatians 2.20)

Acknowledgements

First, I want to acknowledge the debt of gratitude I owe to my parents and to those who were helpful in my initial vocational development. As a questioning teenager exploring faith, I was deeply impressed by the simple holiness of John Clayton, a Roman Catholic priest who showed great hospitality to this young seeker. I am also grateful for the subsequent guidance I received from many priests, some of whom have now died and, in particular, I realize the debt I owe to Richard Buck, Bill Kirkpatrick, Peter Laister and Jim Cotter, and the immense help I received from Brothers Michael and Damian SSF as well as many others, ordained and lay. Outstanding among them was Sister Mary Teresa SLG, a hermit whose care of me as my vocation developed, often chaotically, deepened my desire for God and who introduced me to the riches of the Carmelite tradition.

In putting my thoughts in order, the assistance of a number of people was invaluable, and I am especially grateful for the help I received from the Bishop of Southwark, Sister Sue CSF, Sister Leo OSCl, and the Reverends David D. Anderson and Ed Sniecienski, Fathers Nicholas Cranfield, John Cullen, Neil Evans, Richard Peers SMMS, Paul Symonds and Brett Ward. Their careful reading of various chapters, constructive criticisms and insightful suggestions were extremely helpful as was the discussion I had with a group of clergy attending the Southwark Diocesan IME (Initial Ministerial Education).

I would also like to thank the editorial staff at Canterbury Press for their patience, help and advice to this novice author.

My particular thanks go to someone who wishes to remain anonymous but whose very careful and professional reading and the comments she was able to make were invaluable, as was the help I received from Ann Lewin who proof read the whole book and whose poetry has been inspirational.

The observations of all involved saved me from too many mistakes, and their suggestions as to what was missing and what needed attention were of great help.

Finally, and most importantly, I want to thank Chris, my long-suffering partner, who had to cope with my being shut away in our office for many hours. Without his initial encouragement and ongoing support this book could never have been written.

Foreword

by the Rt Revd Christopher Chessun
Bishop of Southwark

There is much encouragement to be found in these pages. John-Francis has himself 'pondered these things' (as it says in the Ordinal) and shares his insights into the inner life of a priest with great care and beauty. His journey has encompassed the religious life within the Society of St Francis as well as the unpredictability of a parish in east London and has flowed through many decades and different strata, including a secular career in London in which he was drawn to grapple with spiritual questions.

What has now emerged in this book is the distilled wisdom of long experience as a priest, pastor and spiritual director. After drinking deeply himself from the wells of the Tradition, and being fed by them through long and faithful service, John-Francis has now taken up the responsible task of sharing, for the benefit of all making their own journey of faith, the wisdom of the Tradition as he has known it and made it his own.

The Tradition he inherits, distils and passes on is a broadly based one, in which writers and thinkers as various as George Herbert, Maya Angelou and Paul Tillich all have a part to play. But at its heart is the deep hope of humanity this side of eternity, to take the shape which God purposes for each of us, to grow into our true selves, to become the people it is good for us to be.

And within this hope is a sublime paradox: for as our true selves are to be found in Christ alone, and as Christ gave himself up for the sake of others, so to find ourselves is to lose ourselves: 'We are to engage in a constant finding and letting-go of self; a gifting of self and being utterly present to the Other.'

Realizing these possibilities in ourselves is a matter of Grace, and it is a long pilgrimage. There is much food for the journey in this valuable book: much to ponder on, and much to take hold of. I commend it wholeheartedly, and with particular warmth to those who are themselves on a journey of formation. In these pages they will find a fresh but authentic expression of the tradition that has guided God's Church for two thousand years.

The cleanest and most wholesome water is often that which has spent years, perhaps centuries or millennia, seeping out of high mountain glaciers and filtering through rock strata, until at last it issues into the open at the foot of a cliff. I encourage readers to draw real refreshment from these wellsprings.

✝Christopher Southwark

Preface

That in all things, God may be glorified.

(1 Peter 4.11)

❧

'What is that?' enquired the woman on the train pointing to my clerical collar as we sped towards London. Her English was broken and it transpired she was Chinese, and my efforts to explain the collar, the Church and priesthood came to nothing. Given her cultural background, such matters were outside her understanding, yet her simple question set me on a course of reflection on the nature of priestly identity. Others will tell similar stories of brief yet profound encounters: the prayer offered for someone in the street; the confidence received among the supermarket shelves; the confession heard in a pub – the collar still has power to attract and convey something. But just what is it that we *are* conveying as we live out our vocation? I wonder if that simple statement by St Jean-Baptiste-Marie Vianney, the Curé d'Ars, is a simple yet powerful reminder of the heart of our calling:

The priesthood is the love of the heart of Jesus.[1]

The inner life of the priest

This book is concerned with the heart, the inner and often hidden life of a priest. Ministry can be experienced as a never-ending round of 'doing' and, in my experience, the need for simply 'being' can be neglected – usually to the detriment of minister and ministry. Some have noted an apparent conflict between 'being' and 'doing', and similar tensions between the dynamics of secular techniques and gospel values, social activism and spirituality, outreach, contemplation, etc. have been noted. While I don't intend to promote one over the other, experience tells me that if our inner life with God in Christ is ignored or uncared for then, no matter how well things may appear on the surface, there's likely to be trouble ahead.

Why is this book written?

Much of my ministry now is as a spiritual director and, along with others, I often hear priests say they don't have enough time for prayer, so I want to explore how those charged with the care of souls *can* give time to God, not just for their own sake but because if we're to have a heart for evangelization then we also need a heart that's exploring the mysteries of God and God's reign into which we want to draw others.

I think most of us realize how much our inner life determines all that we do, so what's written here is concerned with exploring various aspects of priestly spirituality, some of which may have been forgotten, or are unknown, but which may be of great help, and throughout the chapters you'll find a variety of reflections and suggestions about how we can deepen our spiritual life. It isn't *all* about prayer, but because some avoid its more reflective form – it isn't always easy and can seem rather empty – or even fear what they might have to acknowledge in the silence, each chapter invites you, in different ways, to gaze compassionately on your hidden life as God gazes upon you with divine compassion. They also offer some helps along the way.

I also hope the material you'll find here will help those who have a pastoral care for clergy to consider how their lives set an example of what it means to *be* a deacon or a priest, regardless of where ministry is exercised. I wonder what example they are setting if *they* are rarely seen to pray, seek supervision, engage with spiritual direction or go into retreat? Just because priests appear to be doing wonderful things does not mean that they can neglect prayer. In fact quite the reverse: our hearts need to be awake to the mystery of God in all things so that we may glorify God, as the Benedictine motto I used as the sub-title to this Preface says: '*Ut in Omnibus Glorificetur Dei*' – 'that in all things God may be glorified' (1 Peter 4.11).

Who is this book for?

I hope this book might appeal to people from diverse backgrounds and traditions, and to anyone who might like to know what's going on beneath the role they exercise or see exercised. Reflecting aspects of my own story, it also deals with spiritual direction and pastoral supervision, and it may be of interest to those exercising such ministries as well as those whose priesthood is realized in the workplace.

In writing it, I have become aware that this is probably the book I would like to have read when I was considering ordination. Brought up in a family whose roots lay in non-Conformity and agnostic communism, I chose in my teens to be baptized and confirmed. An interest in the religious life led me to consider joining the Benedictines when I was 20. Later I spent much time with the Carmelite-influenced Sisters of the Love of God at Bede House in Kent, among whom I found, in one of the solitaries, my first spiritual director. But most formative of all were the 25 years I spent as a brother of the Anglican Society of St Francis (SSF), during which I served in kitchens, worked in a prison, ran missions, led youth retreats – and was ordained. My vocation was also informed by that great tradition of Anglican spirituality expressed by people from George Herbert to Michael Ramsey. All this and more (including time with the Coptic Orthodox Church in Egypt) has helped shape my understanding of priestly spirituality reflected in these pages.

What is the purpose of this book?

Many questions arise as one begins to adjust to the calling to the priesthood, and the dynamics of an individual's particular personality and circumstances begin to be affected by one's vocation. Rather than being a self-help guide or instruction manual, this book invites you into an encounter with the Lord as it explores different themes relevant to our inner life. It looks at how the 'grace of priesthood' (a term used by the Revd Donald English, sometime President of the Methodist Conference, when addressing students from my ecumenical ordination training) can be nurtured and deepened. It also offers some resources to help develop one's inner life from the great tradition of spirituality that may be unfamiliar to some.

There are times when priests – good priests – who come for direction find it difficult to talk about their inner relationship with God. Or it becomes clear that, apart from the liturgies they're required to celebrate, their spiritual life has floundered, while some have become slaves to their ministry. Clergy have so many demands made on them that it's easy to neglect the inner life, and the Church sometimes seems more interested in numbers than attending to that life. So three chapters explore prayer and others look at what life in Christ might involve and how we can be helped in our desire for holiness.

Why Jesus?

There's a story found in the *Little Flowers of St Francis* of an encounter between the saint and Brother Masseo, who came to meet Francis after he'd been praying in the woods.

Half-jokingly Masseo asks: 'Why you? Why does everyone run after you, want to see you and hear you and obey you? After all, you are not handsome, or learned, or wise, or rich. So why is all the world running after you?' Francis was very moved by this and prayed for a long time before responding. Then he replied that God had chosen him because he was foolish and sinful, since 'God chose what is foolish in the world to shame the wise; God chose what is weak in the world to shame the strong; God chose what is low and despised in the world, things that are not ... so that no one might boast in the presence of God' (1 Cor. 1.27f.).

These are questions we need to reflect upon: How do I feel about my foolishness? Do I own my own sinfulness or my weakness? Do I care more about what the world thinks of me than of what God sees in me? But Masseo's question could equally be posed to Jesus: '*Why you? Why does everyone run after you?*' And we can also ask ourselves: *Why Jesus? Why do I follow him?* Each of us needs to discover our own answer. For me, it's the way his love embraces me and how his life inspires and challenges me. He is the one I turn to for the forgiveness of my sins, as many and great as they have been, knowing that his compassion for me is boundless.

So this book concerns how we can live *into* our vocation. It's not intended to be prescriptive or exhaustive, nor does it concern what we do so much as who we are in the deep and secret places of the heart. What we do and how we respond to who we encounter *does* inform, sometimes powerfully, who we are and helps us uncover more of that mystery, but, in the end, it's all about Jesus – all *for* Jesus – and I trust it might be of help to you. To that end, I've included some questions at the end of each chapter, which can be used for personal or group reflection. You might like to spend a few moments just recalling what really helps you in your desire to be given to God ...

He is the core of the heart of love,
and He, beyond labouring seas,
our ultimate shore.[2]

ST FRANCIS OF ASSISI *and*
ST IGNATIUS OF LOYOLA

Finally, I'd like to point out that the ordering and dynamic
of the chapters owes something to two saints who, though
separated by 300 years, were clearly brothers in Christ –
Francis of Assisi, born in 1182, and Ignatius of Loyola in
1491 – and who wanted to know themselves in relationship
with him. Ignatius, founder of the Society of Jesus (Jesuits),
wrote the *Spiritual Exercises*, that remarkable 'retreat' that
is such an immense gift to those seeking to make important
life-choices and deepen their life in Christ. And while Francis
didn't write anything similar, there are a number of quotations from the Principles of the Anglican Society of St Francis
– the document that defines its ethos and charism – as appropriate reflections. Each chapter also has suggestions as to
what a priest might need to do to refresh their relationship
with God in Christ.

The chapters reflect the dynamic of the *Exercises*, which,
right at the start, remind us that we need to put a good interpretation on the action of other Christians and not condemn
them (the *Presupposition*) – something to reflect on as we
seek to build on the foundation of our being the beloved of
God. For what matters more than anything else – more than
growing congregations or successful churches – is the quality
of the priest's relationship with God in Christ, which determines everything else, including the way we relate to others.
Like the Principle and Foundation in the *Spiritual Exercises*,
before ever we begin to consider our calling, we must attend

to the way it needs to be rooted in God's utter love for us even though there will be times when we doubt that. As I listen to priests, it's sometimes apparent that this underpinning has been forgotten, ignored or never properly realized, for the hurly-burly of everyday life can wear away any foundation. So before looking at specific matters of concern, the first chapter includes an invitation to relish (as Ignatius would encourage us) God's compassionate love for us. After considering these foundations we'll reflect on how we can deal with our failures through the ministry of Confession before moving on to explore aspects of diaconal life and the needs that are addressed in formational ministries. Then after the chapters on prayer – personal and Eucharistic as well as the place of the Daily Office – we'll consider the resources that can assist our vocation: spiritual direction, supervision, rules of life, retreats, making choices in life, thoughts on being single or called to celibacy, and how we might realize our 'personal vocation'. After considering who we are beneath the role we exercise, we'll look towards the end for which we are made and what part our sexuality has to play as we seek union with the Other.

So, as we begin, let a profound meditation of Francis, which he is said to have used as an all-night prayer, echo in your heart:

'*Who are you, O Lord my God, and who am I?*'

Notes

1 St Jean-Baptiste-Marie Vianney TOSF, Curé d'Ars, *Catechism on the Priesthood*.

2 Sister Janet CSMV, *Mother Jane Margaret CSMV*, St Mary's Press, 1974.

Introduction

In my beginning is my end

❧

'Abide in me as I abide in you.'
(John 15.4)

Much of my ministry at present involves accompanying
people who are seeking to develop their relationship with
Christ through spiritual direction and it is exercised in the
shadow of the Lloyds of London building in the City of
London. Designed by Richard Rogers it excites a variety of
opinions and, like it or loathe it, clearly flies in the face of
Antoine de Saint-Exupéry's famous observation in his book
The Little Prince that 'what is essential is invisible to the eye'.
However, *this* book follows Lord Rogers' desire to expose
what is normally hidden.

Not long ago I sat with a priest recalling her experience of
a diocesan clergy conference when she suddenly exclaimed:
'If I've lost God, what's it all about?' The conference had
offered a breadth of workshops dealing with important
matters – the work of a parish priest in changing times, youth
ministry, church growth, etc. She'd chosen one facilitated by
two Benedictine monks, one Anglican and the other Roman
Catholic, because the subjects they offered spoke to her desire
to deepen her relationship with God, something she knew
she needed to look at in depth. This book is concerned with
exploring that relationship and how it affects what I call
our 'being beneath the role' – the person we are behind the

position we occupy. This needs such care and attention that this book can only attempt to deal with it in a broad way.

All for Jesus

Like every Christian the priest is simply and profoundly called to live out their baptismal vocation. Yet in being a public representative of the Church, a priest is not just representing that body as people see it and may experience it in all its fallibility and brokenness, but also what they see it, however dimly, as having the possibility of being. Priests carry people's hopes, fears, projections – and fantasies. So when the priest visits a sick person, it's not only a kind Christian who is visiting, but one who is seen in a very particular way as a sign of Christ in his mystical body. That can be an uncomfortable thought for some, but it can help us recall that we *are* called to have our heart centred on Jesus, and in humility give thanks when others see him through us.

> We ought not to be weary of doing little things for the love of God, who regards not the greatness of the work but the love with which it is performed. (Brother Lawrence of the Resurrection 1614–91)

&

PRIESTLY SPIRITUALITY?

I don't think there is any spirituality unique to the priesthood, but there are *aspects* of spirituality that have relevance to ministers of word and sacrament, and even the word 'spirituality' itself can be difficult to define. But it can be taken to indicate that which enables us in the depths of our being to desire nothing more than to

Love the Lord your God with all your heart, and with all your soul, and with all your mind (and) your neighbour as yourself. (Matthew 22.37ff.)

It involves the desire we have and the means we employ to respond to the Other, that we might be taken beyond ourselves and deepen our love of God and neighbour through our specific vocational calling to follow Jesus. Whether bishop, priest or deacon, we must all seek to have our hearts remade in his image and likeness: '*The challenge of priestly spirituality is to develop rhythms of living in tune with the Spirit so that the Spirit can animate each aspect of priestly identity and transform the priest into a truly effective person-symbol of Christ.*'[1] There are many specific insights as to how this can be done, and we all have our exemplars in the faith who have highlighted for us aspects of that love of God and neighbour in which we're called to grow in Christ.

The priest as a 'walking sacrament'

It's in the Eucharist that this transformation is most profoundly realized. In a sermon preached in 1968, Austin Farrer, the late Dean of Keble College, Oxford, described the priest as a '*living stem bearing sacraments as its fruit*', for the priest gives us the body and blood of Christ. He went on to say that because the priest bears the sacrament they are themselves sacramental: 'walking sacraments' who through their humanity celebrate and inhabit the words of Christ as they do what he did. I find that a deeply powerful reflection because it reminds me that I occupy a unique, mysterious and holy place. The priest is in some way perceived as the 'threshold-minder' of eternity, not a gatekeeper letting some in and keeping others out (although I've heard of ministers who act as if they had that power), but as one who holds open the door to the mysteries of God. And if I'm not prayerfully exploring that which lies beyond, how can I communicate something of the breadth and length and height and depth of the love of God that surpasses knowledge so that others may be filled with all that fullness (Eph. 3.18ff.)? It's for this reason that we need to remember that while all Christians are called to a life of holiness the priest is called in a particular way, and their faults and failings will be shown up in a particular light.

My vocation

My own sense of being called to the priesthood started to become apparent in 1963, and three years later I joined the pre-theological course run by the Society of the Sacred Mission (SSM) at Kelham, Nottinghamshire. During those studies my sexual identity became known and my bishop refused to recommend me for training. It was a bitter blow, yet 25 years later I was ordained.

Afterwards, I spent six years living out that priestly calling in the context of being a religious, before being released from vows and spending ten years as rector of a 'back-streets' parish on the eastern edge of London. For much of that time I also exercised a ministry of spiritual direction and taught aspects of the subject as well as offering pastoral supervision. All this experience and more forms the context from which this book is written. Through it all, I've come to realize that at the heart of the priesthood there must lie an intentional desire to live out of the loving heart of Christ, and to be inhabited by that creative, compassionate Word.

> *Christ be with me, Christ within me,*
> *Christ behind me, Christ before me,*
> *Christ beside me, Christ to win me,*
> *Christ to comfort and restore me,*
> *Christ beneath me, Christ above me,*
> *Christ in quiet, Christ in danger,*

ENFOLDED IN CHRIST

Christ in hearts of all that love me,
Christ in mouth of friend and stranger.
(St Patrick)

'The Lord's breast is the sponge of the heart.'[2]

Over the years I've come to understand that it's through our immersion in the Heart of Christ, who calls us to follow him, that our calling is most fully realized, and throughout the book reference is made to the 'Heart'. I don't mean the physical organ or the place where our emotions reside, but the central part of our being into which God's Spirit was breathed and which, St John points out, needs to trust in God (John 14.1). Yet it can become corrupted and deceitful, so the Scriptures tell us that we need to guard the heart above all else, for from it flows everything we do: 'Create in me a clean heart, O God; and put a new and right spirit within me' (Ps. 51.10). In the end, Jesus recognizes the need for a 'right' renewed heart when he pronounced the blessedness of those who have a pure heart, for they will see God.

So it is this uncorrupted 'heart' we look to in seeking to explore the priestly life and, while there will always be times when another has our attention, it is to the Heart of God in Christ that we must always turn. And if you're happily married or partnered and worry about any sense of dualism between love of God and love of partner, don't! The two aren't in conflict but complement each other. You can never love God too much, for in turning the eye of your heart to him and allowing love to flow out it will overspill into every other aspect of life. But if a priest allows another to *usurp* the place of God then they are in danger of becoming deaf to their calling, as illustrated in the story of Jesus' call to the rich man who asked to follow him (Mark 10.17f.). Of course, problems can emerge when a partner begins to feel they're playing second fiddle to the Church, so we'll consider that later on.

The compassionate gaze of God

In his *Letter to the Philippians* St Polycarp advised that
'Clergy ... should be (people) of generous sympathies, with
a wide compassion for humanity ... Any show of ill-temper,
partiality, or prejudice is to be ... avoided.' I often notice
the real compassion priests have for those in their care, and
encourage them to realize their compassion as a reflection of
God's, and invite them to consider if any particular account
in the Scriptures might help them to locate their compassion
in a Divine context. Is there an image of God's love that
particularly appeals? The story of Jesus' encounter with a
leper (Luke 17.11f.) reminds us that it is *his* compassionate
gaze we need to hold on to – for we, too, need to sit in that
gaze and hear what it's saying to us. A simple prayer-exercise
for this might be helpful, so one is included in Appendix 1.

Prayer is a demanding practice because it not only requires
us to set aside time for that encounter, but also to face the
multiple distractions that will occur. It will also uncover
layers of our being which we might have ignored, buried or
turned from. So not for nothing are priests expected to pray
the Divine Office each day and to spend time silently gazing
on God, for this is a fundamental aspect of the redemptive
process. How easy it is to slide into living out of the role
rather than the heart of their ever-developing relationship
with Christ. The role might inform that – and, please God,
mould it in creative ways – but it can also hide us from the
heart of our being-in-Christ. The collar can separate us from
ourselves (as well as inviting us to become ourselves), so we
must seek to open ourselves to God's compassionate gaze,
a gaze we might realize when kneeling before the Blessed
Sacrament or facing the suffering of a child in our congregation, meditating on the Scriptures or seeking to aid a
homeless person. What matters is that we allow that contemplative, compassionate gaze and not turn from it while

deepening our realization that it is God's gaze we must nurture in our hearts.

Trinitarian life

Archbishop Welby, speaking to 50 young Anglicans from southern Africa at a conference in 2017, declared: 'I am who I am because I am in Jesus Christ.' His words echo those of the remarkable medieval Franciscan Tertiary, St Catherine of Genoa, who said, 'My self is God, nor is any other self known to me except my God'.[3] The life of the priest is a life lived in the trinity of self, other and God, and, like all Christians, we are to hold this balance while always acknowledging that it is God we seek and who draws us beyond ourselves. It is this mystery of community to which we are called – life, participation, in God (cf. Ps. 82.6; Eph. 1.3–14). And wherever our priesthood is exercised, be it in parish, shop, school, the military or wherever, we must not lose sight of this calling even when we lay down any specific context in which our vocation is exercised.

> *Jesus, may your compassionate love flow into me,*
> *your Mother's heart enfold me*
> *and your suffering and death strengthen me.*
> *For with you close at hand I have nothing to fear.*
> *May the shelter I seek be the shadow of your cross.*
> *Let me not run from the mercy you offer,*
> *but hold me safe from the forces of evil.*
> *On each of my dying's shed your light and your love.*
> *Keep calling to me until that day comes, when,*
> *with your saints,*
> *I may praise you for ever and ever. Amen.*
> (*Prayer of Companions of the Compassionate Hearts of Jesus and Mary, based on the Anima Christi*)

INTRODUCTION

Questions for reflection

- Who is Christ for me?
- How do I nurture my relationship with Christ and how might this need to be enriched that others may find him through who I am? What of Christ might they notice through me? What needs more attention?
- Is there anything about myself that needs to be opened to Christ's compassionate gaze?

Notes

1 R. Hauser, 'Priestly Spirituality', in P. Fink (ed.), *The New Dictionary of Sacramental Worship*. Liturgical Press, 1991, p. 1024. [© by Order of Saint Benedict. Liturgical Press, Collegeville, Minnesota. Used with permission.]

2 St Gregory of Nyssa, *Commentary on the Song of Songs*.

3 *Spiritual Doctrine of St Catherine of Genoa*, ch. XIV.

I

What Do You Seek?

A passion for God

In the name of our Lord we bid you remember the great-ness of the trust that is now to be committed to your charge. Remember always with thanksgiving that the treasure now to be entrusted to you is Christ's own flock, bought by the shedding of his blood on the cross. It is to him that you will render account for your stewardship of his people. (Ordination of Priest: The Declarations)

O God, you are my God, for you I long;
For you my soul is thirsting.
My body pines for you
Like a dry, weary land without water.
(Psalm 62.1)

It was the summer of '65, the Rolling Stones were 'Top of the Pops' and *The Sound of Music* had just been released to rapturous audiences. I was 19, newly confirmed and a deeply enthusiastic Christian for whom the faith blazed out and con-sumed all else. A year later, I read a novel called *The Cardinal* and to say I was inspired would be an understatement. The book concerns one man's struggle with a vocation to the priesthood and the heroic way he eventually lived that out in the slums of New York, an account which awoke the seed of my own calling. Years later, I discovered that St Ignatius had

had a similar experience when reading the lives of Sts Francis and Dominic, to which his response had been: 'If they can do such things, so can I!' Thus began the story of my – long and somewhat tortuous – journey to priesthood. Others will have their own. But what is common for all priests, I trust, is that we have a sense of being called into an ever-deepening relationship with the Lord who graciously shares with us his vocation.

ॐ

OUR PRIMARY CALLING

Life has taken me along many and varied paths where people and places have been formative, not least during 25 years of Franciscan religious life and the subsequent time as a parish priest. On first joining the Anglican Franciscans, I came across some words by the then Minister General, Br Geoffrey SSF. He asked a group of novices, as had St Benedict the founder of Western monasticism, to consider why they had come – a question equally applicable to any consideration of the priesthood. Was it because they thought Franciscans preached well and ran good missions? Or because they felt a need for community? Or were sickened and alarmed by the world? Or wanted to help people in need?

'It is not wrong', he went on to say, *'to have any or all of these motives in your mind as you come and seek to join us. It may be that in being here all these things will be achieved. But not one of these is entirely adequate as a motive. There is one motive which must be over and above all these subsidiary motives and which must be your consuming passion if you are to become a true Friar: I come to seek God.' ('Vocation', SSF)*

Now I realize that reflection concerning our primary calling to seek God also applies to all Christians, but the priest, like the religious, is looked upon as someone who has made an *explicit* response to share their life with Jesus (Mark 3.13; cf. John 17.24). However, do you notice the way that calling can become buried by either the role we have or the work we do? Many of those exercising the ministry of spiritual direction have come to realize the need many have to rediscover their primary, personal vocation.

The 'personal vocation'

I love the description of human life as the 'vocation to faithfulness'.[1] But, for many, vocation is normally considered in relation to the outward expression of a particular ministry: '[A vocation is a] particular calling to serve God and all people through one of the Church's authorized lay or ordained ministries'.[2] It's also often understood in terms of a call to live the religious life or a 'lay' vocation to nursing, teaching, medicine etc. But in his book *Discovering Your Personal Vocation*, Herbert Alphonso SJ goes further. He writes about the importance of discovering our 'primary calling',[3] which lies at the heart of who we are and is utterly unique to each of us. It's that vocation which we're to live out whether we find ourselves in parishes, schools, offices or wherever. God has written it on the palm of his hand (Isa. 49.16), and as we listen deeply to him we realize our calling. Emerging from the 'core-self', it's deeper than any ministerial vocation but gives it life and meaning. When I first heard these wonderful words of St Jean-Baptiste-Marie Vianney, 'the priesthood is the love of the heart of Jesus', they resonated in a place which I now realize is where that 'personal vocation' is heard.

To the greater glory of God

As that sense of vocation develops and we enter into the process of testing that call through training and initial formation, the foundations of our faith will be exposed, an experience that can be very hard for some. From time to time, I sit with ordinands who are going through this 'stripping' and have to assure them that this is quite normal and, in the end, it's in order that their lives might reveal the glory of God in Christ (cf. 2 Cor.13.5). As tough as it may be, welcome this stripping! Yes, the journey will be hard and painful at times, and as the foundations of our faith are tested it may become apparent that they're rooted more on external supports (Scripture, tradition, the witness of others, etc.) than on Christ. If our faith is determined by externals, whether Scripture or the Church, we'll need to embark on a process of owning it for ourselves. At this moment we need to realize God's utter love for us and deepen our desire to return that love as the old is stripped away that the new might emerge. Prayer is one of the places where this needs to be done as we present our confusions to God, holding on to the simple fact that we are loved and precious in God's sight. Growing is a painful process (1 Cor. 13.11), and it takes time! Many years ago, my confessor told me to be patient with the process, keep to a simple rule of prayer and don't get trapped by despair if entering into a period of confusion. You may be tempted to return to the certainties of spiritual childhood, but they may have to be left behind if we are to be of use to others. God calls us on a vocational pilgrimage where we must leave the known for the unknown if we are to grow into Christ. What matters is what God is doing in the heart, something the psalms, especially 139, so often express.

Of course, the 'core-self', the heart of who we are, is where the image of God is to be discovered (Gen. 2.7; 2 Cor. 3.3). From that place all true spirituality emerges as water gushes up from the depths of a well (John 4.7–15). Ignatius Loyola, in his *Spiritual Exercises*, recalls the foundational importance of this place where the love of God is to be known, saying that 'God created human beings to praise, reverence, and serve God and be happy with him forever.' Behind all he wrote and lived was the desire that life should be lived 'to the greater glory of God' – *Ad Maiorem Dei Gloriam (AMDG)* – which he took as his motto. This is what you and I were created for, and it is when we are living out of that expression of praise that we're most fully human.

> *I love you, Lord, my strength,*
> *my rock, my fortress, my saviour.*
> *My God is the rock where I take refuge;*
> *my shield, my mighty help, my stronghold.*
> *(Psalm 18.1f.)*

Ignatius also observes that that foundation needs to be firm if it is to support our journey with God into the fullness of our being, something that must be particularly true for those in ministry. We need to accept that, sinners though we are, we're loved by the God who made us in his image and likeness. Sadly, what happened during their formative years means that some people are not sure, deep within, that they *are* loved. And if you had to 'earn' the love of another, no wonder there will be some, charged with telling the story of God's unconditional love, who will not have the certainty of that and who will preach that it's conditional. It isn't of course. It's unconditional; it's all grace.

The wounded healer

Because of the abuse they suffered when they were young, some people find this godly, unconditional love hard to accept. Indeed, their notion of love itself might have been profoundly

marred. Others may have been scarred by constantly failing to live up to the expectations of parents or might have
experienced rejection by peers. We all know that abuse comes
in many forms – physical, emotional, sexual or spiritual – but
all involve misuses of power and many have to live with deep,
and sometimes hidden, wounds, wounds for which it might
be difficult to find complete healing. But, apart from our need
to address any such forms of abuse through the appropriate
channels, it can also become a source of healing for others.
Much of our life in Christ involves the acceptance of our
woundedness, seeking appropriate means of healing and then
allowing that place of woundedness to be the place where
compassion grows. The wounded priest can be a real witness
to Christ, the wounded healer, if we can allow the pain we
carry to be transformed into compassion for others and begin
to trust them as we trust God. This can be a long and difficult process, but therapeutic ministries, including spiritual
ones, can provide great help. We'll look at some of those in
Chapter 8.

Unfortunately, there are those who, for whatever reason,
hide their wounds. Clergy, in particular, may be tempted to
put on an act or wear a mask to show the world a 'happy
face'. But it can be a face concealing insecurity, depression,
emptiness in the heart, etc. Although we're called to live
'to the greater glory of God', some of us act out a life that
drives us harshly to the point where our humanity becomes
obscured. If a priest recognizes this is happening to them and
they're beginning to develop a hardened approach to life,
they can explore this with a spiritual director, for such a face
often hides deep pain.

In a similar way, there are pastors who are quite hard on
others, always believing they are right and keen to impose
their will: such people are difficult taskmasters, both to others
and themselves. I hope they're able, like all of us, to feel that
compassionate gaze of God and to learn humility, something

we'll be exploring. Sadly, there are curates or parishioners who are bullied by their vicar, who believes he or she has a hotline to God. In cases like this, they might be encouraged to turn to the appropriate channels to address this form of abuse. We all need to remember that at the end of our days we shall not be judged by our success or how many souls we've saved, by our popularity, erudition, intelligence or whatever but, as St John of the Cross is reputed to have said, 'by our loving'.

❧

DRAWN BY LOVE

The compassionate Heart of Jesus

One of the greatest images that reminds us of this truth, that speaks to everyone of love, is the image of the heart, and the Church is fortunate in having a particular image of the heart that speaks of God's everlasting, compassionate love: the Sacred Heart. It may be unfamiliar to some non-Catholics, a bit too 'Roman' perhaps, but did you know that the Sacred Heart inspired John Wesley, whose conversion experience began when his own heart was 'deeply warmed'? Or that the founders of the first Franciscan community for men in the Church of England dedicated their community to the Divine Compassion – another way of speaking of the Sacred Heart? One of its founding members, Fr Andrew SDC (1869–1946), wrote this gentle meditation:

To rest a tired head upon Thy Heart,
And to be still –
To come to Thee from the whole world apart
And learn Thy Will –
And in that will, because it is Thy will, to live and die,

Knowing Thy love and will are one eternally.
That be my way of prayer –
that brings me where Thou art –
Heaven is there.[4]

The heart of the matter

It's of primary importance that we seek to be aware of, and in touch with, the heart of who we are, for the inner life of the priest will determine everything. The Oracle at Delphi is reputed to have said that the greatest wisdom is to 'know thyself', but that can be quite challenging. I recall becoming very angry when I first began to reflect on those words because they suggested I needed to face up to aspects of myself I'd been avoiding and was now trying to get rid of. This self-awareness can awaken at any time so, to make sure that any distraction we might experience isn't too overwhelming, we always need to consider the inclination of our heart. Is it directed towards the Heart of the One who desires us and who will always love us? Or something else? As a Benedictine monk once said to someone exploring their vocation: 'Brother, you must make your stability in the Heart of Jesus.'[5] That's worth chewing on: Christ must be the heart of the priest's heart whether that priest be celibate, single or partnered. If he isn't, other loves can easily move in to occupy the void.

There's a story told of a priest in Africa who was translating St John's Gospel into the local dialect. There were many problems in finding the right way to translate some of the English words, one such being to 'believe'. There was no exact word in the dialect. So he asked one of the locals for help and, after hearing the priest explain what the word meant, the man said 'To believe means to listen with the heart.' That's what the priest is called to do. 'What is God doing with your heart?' is the question that sometimes gets asked in spiritual direction for, as the potter shapes the clay into its desired shape and form, can there be any greater desire for the priest than that their heart might be re-formed into the Heart of Jesus? In a sermon to priests in 2016, Pope Francis said:

> *The Heart of the Good Shepherd is not only the Heart that shows us mercy, but is itself mercy. There the Father's love shines forth; there I know I am welcomed and understood as I am; there, with all my sins and limitations, I know the certainty that I am chosen and loved. Contemplating that Heart, I renew my first love: the memory of that time when the Lord touched my soul and called me to follow him, the memory of the joy of having cast the nets of our life upon the sea of his word.' (cf. Luke 5.5) ... Contemplating the Heart of Christ we are faced with the fundamental question of our priestly life: Where is my heart directed?* It is a question we need to keep asking, daily, weekly ... *Where is my heart directed? Our ministry is often full of plans, projects and activities: from catechesis to liturgy, to works of charity, to pastoral and administrative commitments. Amid all these, we must still ask ourselves: What is my heart set on?* ... Where is it directed, what is the treasure that it seeks? For as Jesus says: *'Where your treasure is, there will your heart be also.' (Matthew 6.21)*[6]

———

Divine Compassion must be the aroma of the priest.[7]

Jesus, our Great High Priest

Our contemplation of him who was given the dignity of priest-hood (Heb. 8.4–6) reminds us that we must 'refer all good to the Lord God most High and Supreme; let us acknowledge that all good belongs to Him, and let us give thanks for all to Him from whom all good proceeds'.[8] Our calling is to proclaim him who is the 'reflection of God's glory', so we are to be known as women and men living lives of great and deep thankfulness, who, at the end of our days, will come before him who is our friend, brother, judge and saviour. We'll be delving further into this later on.

At the end of our days

Priests, of all people, need to keep their eyes fixed on the goal they desire, as the writer of the Letter to the Hebrews reminds us (12.2). There are people who can exercise many important ministries but, as we've noted, the priest's attention needs to be focused on God to whom we'll be called to render account at the end of our days. So in a real way, we must set one foot on this side of eternity *and* one foot on the other. Called to live in the poverty of Christ who emptied himself of himself, abandoning his life to death, we need to hold lightly to the things of this earth and seek to store up for ourselves treasures in heaven. This is what we must keep in mind (Phil. 2.5): our deepest security, the foundation on which all else is built, is to be found in that awareness of being the beloved of God.

All this is disclosed most fully in the Eucharist. As stewards of that great Mystery, priests have the tremendous privilege of standing where Christ is 'at the right hand of God' (Heb. 8.1). Called also to show forth his glory in the 'here and now of life', they inhabit the role of the One who presides at the Supper of the Lamb, that eternal Liturgy which is not ours to celebrate but his.

Are you in charge of a parish? If so, do not neglect the parish of your own soul, do not give yourself to others so completely that you have nothing left for yourself. You have to be mindful of your people without becoming forgetful of yourself. (St Charles Borromeo 1538–84)

So we're to live out of thankfulness – (*eucharistia*) – until our lives become one hymn of praise. I was privileged to know a great Franciscan brother, Bill Lash,[9] who, on his deathbed, simply said: 'Rejoice' before dying. When he was nearing death, St Francis said to his brothers, 'I have done what was mine to do; may Christ teach you what you are to do.' We place great emphasis on the start of a ministry; we are prepared for it, trained for it, and the Induction or Licensing service in the Church of England is usually lengthy, solemn and rich in meaning. But isn't it striking that, even after decades of liturgical revision, no liturgies have been created for the close of a ministry? So as no formal service has been produced, a Liturgy for *Praying Our Farewells* is included in Appendix 2. In my beginning is my end.

It's natural that every priest hopes to look back on a ministry and see signs of fruitfulness, hoping their role will be recognized and, maybe, celebrated. But regardless of that we should never forget how 'success' in these terms is not quite what Jesus had in mind. Nor that when he died only his mother, one disciple and a couple of friends remained at his side. His declaration 'It is accomplished!' invites us to consider what we wish to 'accomplish'? We can do no better than turn to the Great High Priestly (Farewell) Prayer of Jesus (John 17.1–26) to realize what he gave thanks for as we meditate on his declaration that the 'hour has come' (17.1), that 'hour' which was prophesied in his very first Sign at Cana which foreshadowed that Supper when he revealed the new wine of the age to come. In his book, *Markings*, Dag Hammarskjöld, Secretary-General of the United Nations until his untimely death in 1961, records some simple words with a profoundly Eucharistic undertone, which many would take for their own: 'For all that has been, thanks. For all that shall be, yes.'

'*In my beginning is my end ... in my end is my beginning.*' Even as a ministry begins, it is our end that needs to inform us. Ministers of the Gospel need to remember and hold on to St Paul's striking assertion: 'If for this life only we have hoped in Christ, we are of all people most to be pitied' (1 Cor. 15.19). Wherever we're on the path to God, we should never forget that we're called to seek union with him whose loving desire for us never ceases (Lam. 3.23).

Accustom yourself continually to make many acts of love,
for they enkindle and melt the soul.
(St Teresa of Avila)

Questions for reflection

- How am I responding to God's invitation to sit in His compassionate gaze? In what ways might I need to give that greater attention?
- What gives meaning and life to my vocation? What was it about Jesus that attracted me? What image of him might now emerge in my heart? Is there any other person in Scripture or among the saints who resonates with my sense of vocation?
- For what am I thankful? What do I sense I am called to 'accomplish'? How does this relate to the gospel? To what, as a priest, do I 'look forward'?

Notes

1 Edward Schillebeeckx, *Christ the Sacrament of the Encounter with God*, Rowman & Littlefield, 1963, p. 13.
2 *Vocation – Do You Have a Calling?*, https://churchsupporthub. org/vocations/about-vocations/exploring-your-vocation.
3 Herbert Alphonso, *Discovering Your Personal Vocation: The Search for Meaning through the Spiritual Exercises*, Paulist Press, 2001.
4 *The Poems of Fr. Andrew SDC*, Mowbray, 1950.
5 '*Frère, tu dois faire ta stabilité dans le Coeur de Jésus*', spoken

in1975 by Dom Nathanaël Carron de La Morinais OSB at the Sacro Speco of Subiaco Abbey, Italy, to Dom Mark Daniel Kirby OSB.

6 Homily on Jubilee of Mercy for Priests, 3 June 206, https://w2.vatican.va/content/francesco/en/homilies/2016/documents/papa-francesco_20160603_omelia-giubileo-sacerdoti.html (© Libreria Editrice Vaticana).

7 The author.

8 *First Rule of St Francis*, 1221.

9 Bill Lash (1905–86) had, along with Fr Jack Winslow and Fr Algy SSF, been a member of the first Anglo-Indian ashram, the *Christa Prema Seva* (Community of the Servants of Christ), in Pune, India, before moving to the UK where he lived at Hilfield Friary.

2

Still I Rise

Confession, Absolution and Reconciliation

Formed by the word, they are to call their hearers to repentance and to declare in Christ's name the absolution and forgiveness of their sins. (Ordination of Priests: The Declarations)

> *Have mercy on me, O God,*
> *according to your merciful love;*
> *according to your great compassion,*
> *blot out my transgressions.*
> *Wash me completely from my iniquity,*
> *and cleanse me from my sin.*
> *(Psalm 51.3–4)*

Broken

We're probably very aware that in spite of the call we have, the desire we embrace and our will to accomplish much, we fail; something St Paul knew only too well:

> *I do not understand my own actions. For I do not do what I want, but I do the very thing I hate. Now if I do what I do not want, I agree that the law is good. But in fact it is no longer I that do it, but sin that dwells within me. For I know that nothing good dwells within me, that*

is, in my flesh. I can will what is right, but I cannot do it. For I do not do the good I want, but the evil I do not want is what I do. (Romans 7.16–20)

Doubtless we're also only too conscious of the brokenness of our world, which is clearly not as God created it to be, and part of our task is to help with that ministry of reconciliation and restoration to help undo the work of the evil one (Matt. 13.19). But neither, of course, are we as God created us to be. We're broken people, broken priests who need to take the log out of our own eye before we try to take the splinter out of the eye of another.

෨

RANSOMED, HEALED, RESTORED, FORGIVEN

Christ's sufferings

The more we realize God's love for us, a love even to death, the clearer we see ourselves and the sharper become the shadows cast by our sin. So as part of our developing relationship with God, the priest, like any other Christian, needs to prayerfully consider how Jesus came to earth *for me*; how he suffered *for me* and died *for me*. Julian of Norwich, the great fourteenth-century mystic, was given a wonderful insight into this in the ninth revelation she received and wrote of in her book, *Revelations of Divine Love*.[1] This concerned the joy God has in suffering and dying for us, and that if he could have done more he would have. She realized God's love is the foundation of our life in Christ and that that love enfolds, embraces and completely surrounds us and will never be taken from us. For God is all that is good, she writes,[2] and in God's compassionate gaze we can own the truth of our own being – warts and all. That's the starting point of this book.

Held in Love's embrace

Many hope that by embracing a new life, a life given to God, the wounds and sins they carry – whether their own or the sin done to them, the painful memories of hurt and abuse, which can be locked away in a deep recess of the heart for so long – will, somehow, disappear. They hope that they can escape from their burden.

But we know differently. As someone who carried such a burden and struggled for so long with 'disordered desires', I realize we can never escape our past. But the past *can*, with tender care, prayer, mercy, love and, when necessary, confession, be redeemed. The past makes us who we are, but a redeemed past makes us who we are *in Christ*. I still remember the wonder with which I read words given me when I was beginning my life as a Franciscan:

> *Oh, the comfort*
> *the inexpressible comfort of feeling safe with a person;*
> *having neither to weigh thoughts nor measure words,*
> *but pouring them all right out, just as they are,*
> *chaff and grain together;*
> *certain that a faithful hand will take and sift them,*
> *keep what is worth keeping,*
> *and then with the breath of kindness blow the rest away.*[3]

So it is that the priest is called to exercise not only a ministry of compassion and mercy but one of forgiveness and absolution. The Rite of Ordination does not mention that, in accompanying others, our own wounds and brokenness will be revealed. Nonetheless, it's clear that as we go on, we'll discover *our* need of healing and wholeness, masked though that might be. For this reason, those of us who have a pastoral care for others need to consider how Confession plays a part in our lives.

The greatest Love

I've long known that I am a sinner. Like John Newton, the eighteenth-century Anglican priest and founder of the evangelical Clapham Sect, I've experienced shame and confusion and realize my need for the 'amazing grace' of forgiveness.[4] The first glimmers of my own vocation when I was 17 were accompanied by a great desire to be washed clean of my sin (Ps. 51.4). I'd been baptized and was considering confirmation when I became aware, quite suddenly, of the way sin lodged in me (and for me that concerned 'sins of the flesh' because, in those days, even *being* gay was regarded as sinful). I longed for a way to be rid of that burden. I'd just begun my working life in the City of London in an office located across the road from a Wren church and, in my new-found keenness, decided one lunchtime to look inside. Maybe pray. But I was confused; incense, statues and the Book of Common Prayer seemed odd bedfellows. But there was a sense of Presence and Mystery that drew me back. One of the things that caused me to return – for I had seen nothing like it before, except in Roman Catholic churches, which I sometimes scurried into – was the life-sized Crucifix opposite the entrance. As I stood before it, I was instantly and surprisingly struck by the sense that he died for *me*. 'Such love', it said to me, such love.

Next to the crucifix I noticed what appeared to be a large cupboard with a seat in the centre and curtains on either side which I later discovered was a Confessional. Eventually, I entered it to make my First Confession. Kneeling before a priest and off-loading all my sins (under the 'seal' of confidentiality) was a remarkable experience, an 'unloading', a shedding of the burden of my sins of thought, word and deed. I knew there must be a penance and that I was not absolved from the consequences of any misbehaviour. Quite the contrary.

Our Lord Jesus Christ, who has left power to his Church
to absolve all who truly repent and believe in him,
of his great mercy forgive you your offences;
and by his authority committed to me,
I absolve you ✠ from all your sins,
in the name of the Father, and of the Son, and of the Holy
Spirit. Amen.

Penitence means that I own my sin, promise with God's help not to sin again, accept my guilt, express contrition and desire to repent. Confessing one's sins is not about having it all swept under the carpet; it's about being honest to another and, as a consequence, to oneself.

Over the years I've discovered confessors who've accepted me with mercy and found, in the Confessional, a place where I rediscover God's loving gaze piercing through all my conflicting desires. I continue to value and recognize my need to make a regular confession of my sin, often 'small' and of apparently little consequence. Nevertheless, I find that 'still I rise', as the black American poet Maya Angelou wrote in her poem of that name, and find it a real gift of grace and liberation, as well as believing it my duty as a Christian and as a priest to make my Confession.

Sadly in some churches the Confessional has now become the broom cupboard.

THE SACRAMENT OF CONFESSION

'All may; none must; some should'

We know that practice of 'making your Confession' fell out of general use after the Reformation, but some did continue to teach its value and necessity. John Overall, a post-Reformation Bishop of Norwich, wrote:

Venial sins that separate not from the grace of God need not so much to trouble a man's conscience; if he hath committed any mortal sin, then we require Confession of it to a Priest, who may give him, upon his true contrition and repentance, the benefit of Absolution, which takes effect according to his disposition that is absolved.[5]

While Confession is *not* the same as therapy, there are similarities, not least in the matter of needing to admit what lies deepest in my heart to another who is bound by rules of confidentiality. Where it *differs* is that it's not, primarily, about who the person is (that is the matter of spiritual direction); rather, it's about the ability of the sacrament to release a person from the chains of sin. Sadly, that well-rehearsed Anglican dictum, 'All may, none must, some should', has diverted attention from the real means of personal conversion and grace offered by this sacrament, which has become yet another of the Church of England's 'best kept secrets'. Sometimes I want to say to the Church, 'Wake up! You've a great gift to offer, something of practical value.' But it needs her ministers to realize and teach the importance of this sacrament. Every priest is called to preach repentance, and I know some will say that people are invited to consider this at the beginning of each Eucharist, but is the General Confession and Absolution really an adequate response for those who need to repent?

Evangelicals and Confession

In his book, *The Cost of Discipleship*, Dietrich Bonhoeffer wrote about what he called 'cheap grace', which he described as preaching forgiveness without repentance and absolution without personal confession; grace without discipleship, the cross and Jesus Christ. Yet some Christians are concerned about the notion of confessing to a priest, maintaining that only Christ has the power to absolve. Which is correct, the priest only *declares* the reconciliation that Christ obtained for us and entrusted to his disciples; it's not the priest's absolution, nor does any power they might have secure forgiveness and reconciliation. While it's true that the sacrament must be celebrated by a priest, they're only 'necessary' as officiant, not as the person with the power in and of themselves to forgive or absolve. That power is Christ's and Christ's alone.

In an article in the *Daily Telegraph* on 9 October 2013 Archbishop Welby wrote:

> *It is enormously powerful and hideously painful when (confession) is done properly ... it's really horrible when you go to see your confessor – I doubt you wake up in the morning and think, this is going to be a bunch of laughs. It's really uncomfortable. But through it God releases forgiveness and absolution and a sense of cleansing.*

And John Newton is reputed to have observed:

> *We can easily manage if we will only take, each day, the burden appointed to it. But the load will be too heavy for us if we carry yesterday's burden over again today, and then add the burden of the morrow before we are required to bear it.*

How true.

My chains fell off

The juxtaposition of the Crucifix and Confessional in that church in the City was not accidental, for in realizing the love that Jesus has for me, a sinner, my response was to fall at his feet and seek forgiveness. And as I heard the words of Absolution, I experienced in my heart and in my body that sense of elation which burdened Christian experienced in John Bunyan's book *The Pilgrim's Progress* when he comes to the 'place of deliverance' (the Cross) and the straps which had tied his great load of sin were cut from his back. I, like Christian, left that Confessional with a tremendous sense of joy, feeling that my life had been restored. Since then, that same sense of my 'chains falling off' accompanies the Absolution I receive. I will, I know, need to turn and turn again; to live a life of repentance as I seek to be open to the truth of who I am before God.

The prodigal returns

While there are many references in the Scriptures to the need for forgiveness and reconciliation, the most powerful image that has moved people to make their Confession is probably that of the return of the Prodigal, also called the Parable of the Loving Father. The one who 'came to himself', who decided to 'rise' from the filth of his life and return to his father, admit his mistakes and ask to be accepted home. The parable contains two telling phrases.

The first is that simple statement: *'he came to himself'*. When I sin, I know I'm 'not myself'. To be 'myself' in religious terms means to live in the freedom that comes as I seek at-one-ness with God. The phrase has also been translated as 'he came to his senses', had the courage to own himself. And that's hard! I have come to realize that one of the most powerful aspects of the Confessional is the way we have to admit something to another human being. I find the way we use that word 'admit' to describe both letting something out *and* allow something in quite fascinating, but maybe you've already realized that. By making my Confession, I open my heart to God and allow another human being to see inside me. While it's easy to admit something in the silence of my heart, it's quite different to hear myself say it aloud to another person.

The other concerns the time when the repentant son turns to home and Jesus says, 'But while he was still far off, *his father saw him and was filled with compassion;* ran and put his arms around him and kissed him' (Luke 15.20). The deep compassion that the father had for his son was – and is – activated as the son makes that first step to return. God is looking for our return; he will bless all who seek forgiveness for their sins, who seek reconciliation, not least through this sacramental means.

What happens in Confession?

Confessions are heard in different ways and places; some-times formal, sometimes not; whatever necessity dictates. I think it's good to have a recognized place in church where Confessions are heard, like the font for baptism and altar for the Eucharist, but they can happen anywhere. One of the most powerful I made was at Taizé where a dozen or so priests stood around the walls of the appropriately named Church of Reconciliation hearing the Confessions of hundreds of young people. Confessions can be made from the comfort of an armchair, kneeling in a sitting room, at a prie-dieu or in the traditional box. And the words will vary according to the context, although the format – Confession with contrition, a desire to amend and words of Absolution (sometimes formal, sometimes not) – won't. It can also be appropriate to suggest or offer symbolic acts, such as laying hands on the penitent as Absolution is pronounced.

Back to what happens! Traditionally the penitent kneels before the priest who encourages them by saying words like:

The Lord be in your heart and on your lips that you may rightly and truly confess your sins, in the name of the Father, and of the Son ✠ and of the Holy Spirit.

Making your Confession – being open and honest – may be a blessing in disguise, but it's a costly blessing. After all, sin has a price.

And with such encouragement the penitent begins to open their heart:

> *I confess to almighty God*
> *and before the whole company of heaven,*
> *that I have sinned through my own fault,*
> *in my thoughts and in my words,*
> *in what I have done and in what I have failed to do.*

But, hang on, someone will say, 'I don't need to confess to anyone except God, and I certainly don't need to confess to the saints!' Well, that's true – to an extent. The problem is that sin isn't a personal matter between me and God; sin disrupts the fabric of the universe. Like throwing stones into a pond, the ripples of sin disturb life, and not just on the surface. My sin affects earth and heaven, if you like, and I need to acknowledge that and realize that the effects of what I do 'in my thoughts and in my words, in what I have done and in what I have failed to do' can be far wider than I might realize. It's the 'Kicking the Cat' syndrome.

And we can't always make amends for our sin. Sometimes we can apologize to the 'cat', or ask forgiveness of someone, do something to right a wrong and so on. But many times it's impossible to right all the consequences of what we've done, even if we are aware of them. So the penitent ends their Confession with the words:

> *For these and all the other sins that I cannot remember I*
> *am heartily sorry, firmly mean to do better, most humbly*
> *ask pardon of God and of your penance (advice) and*
> *absolution. Amen.*

Contrition for what we have done and a real desire to amend one's life must be part of the process. Confession isn't just about finding forgiveness; it's about desiring to change one's heart and the way one lives.

Confession and conversion

So the sacrament recognizes our need to practise 'continuous conversion' of the heart. 'We should continue to turn to God as children, being continuously converted every day of our lives.'[6] If we, ministers of Christ and children of God, are to help turn others to Christ then the centre of *our* being – our heart – needs to be constantly refocused into Christ: 'Blessed are the pure in heart, for they shall see God.' The Faith we preach is all about that gentle reordering of the whole of our being – my being – in Christ until my heart becomes his, a process which will reveal our need to be freed from those influences that draw the heart of who we are from God and God's reign. 'Truly I tell you, unless you change and become like children, you will never enter the kingdom of heaven' (Matt. 18.3). Through the use of this sacrament, we open our hearts to the Beatitudes, ask that our failings be forgiven and acknowledge our need to be converted to the reign of God. To confess our sins to God is not to admit anything God doesn't already know but to admit to *ourselves* what *we* need to know and have the slate wiped clean.

While it's important that clergy don't neglect their duty of explaining the place of Confession in the life of a Christian, they must also witness to the cost of this ministry. Making the practice of Confession part of life will help in realizing this means of grace as we seek to fulfil our calling to 'reconcile the world to Christ' (2 Cor. 5.17–19).

No one will come!

Even though there's no reason not to, and many reasons why they should, few Anglican churches advertise set times for Confession (and that applies especially to our cathedrals, which are visited by so many needy individuals). I don't believe that the thought 'no one might come' is a good enough reason why a time need not be advertised. It can always provide space when the priest can engage in some reading, for example, or it might provide that 'time for God' many want. And all priests need to be ready to hear a Confession, formal or informal, as The Order for the Visitation of the Sick in the Book of Common Prayer makes clear, just as they need to be ready to offer any other means of healing of which this Sacrament is an example.

Trained and prepared

But if we're to hear Confessions, we need some training and if that's not provided, an experienced confessor can always be approached for guidance. If you're going to hear them on a regular basis, you'll also need to check if your bishop expects their priests to obtain permission. And, don't forget, those who offer this ministry need to be regular penitents. In *The Christian Priest Today*, Michael Ramsey reminded clergy of the importance of having a 'technical grasp' of the process and what words to use 'quietly and decisively ... being calm, serene and, in the true sense, "business-like"'.[7] And to make sure that, providing the penitent expresses contrition, Absolution *is* pronounced. Through the priest, God forgives the guilt and removes the eternal punishment associated with sin, providing the penitent says that they mean to amend their ways, are contrite and seek absolution. These three elements need to be included in whatever formula is used.

Penance, advice and absolution

I've often noticed that the 'advice' I've been given has not necessarily touched on the matter that took most of my attention and about which I had a deep sense of guilt and shame as I prepared for and made my Confession. What *has* often been focused on is my relationship, or lack of it, with Christ, and the wisest words I've often received concern how I need to attend to that relationship. But Absolution isn't dependent on the penitent asking for 'advice', although if they don't ask for a penance then it would be appropriate to gently notice how that request has not been made.

Doing one's penance isn't what 'earns' our forgiveness; what matters is that the person also admits to wanting to amend their ways. It's really important that this is recognized and noted, and the penance offered (a psalm or prayer) should help focus on that desire and needs to be something that can be performed soon after the dismissal. For example, if the penitent has expressed an awareness of selfishness in relation to their partner then Psalm 34 can be helpful, or Psalm 13 if someone needs to be reassured that God hasn't forgotten them. Psalm 136 speaks of God's enduring mercy; 92, 96 and 98 of thankfulness. If you're like me, you'll need to develop a book of scriptural cribs for the Confessional! It's a small act of thankful discipline to assist our growth in holiness.

The 'seal' of the Confessional

Finally, we need to remember that, unlike other forms of confidential ministry, 'what's said in the Confessional stays in the Confessional'. It is protected by law, and the priest is forbidden (by the unrepealed Proviso to Canon 113 of the Code of 1603) to reveal or make known to any person what has been confessed. This requirement of absolute confidentiality applies even after the death of the penitent (the 'seal of the Confessional') and even if matters of grave concern are admitted unless 'they be such crimes as by the laws of this realm his own life may be called into question for concealing the same'. It's a burden the confessor must carry, although they might seek advice provided that was confidential and anonymous.

Devotional Confessions

If they think about it at all, people will probably think of Confession only in terms of 'mortal' sins (not that the Church of England any longer classifies sins). Many are drawn to make a 'devotional' Confession as part of their personal, spiritual discipline. Michael Ramsey pointed out that some Christians will use this sacrament as they seek to 'grow in holiness',[8] and the practice of making your Confession on a regular basis can help in the development of humility. Some find that the practice of regular, say bi-monthly, spiritual direction seems to obviate the need for Confession, yet that is to miss the point of realizing that we are 'sinners in need of a saviour'. So some will see the need to make their Confession from time to time, possibly before the great Festivals.

Confession and spiritual direction

I don't think the sacrament should be confused with spiritual direction. Being asked for 'advice' in the Confessional shouldn't result in a sermonette; rather, the words should be brief, kindly, empathic and comforting – in the true meaning of that word. It's been said that the role of the confessor can be likened to that of a father and mother, physician, teacher – and judge. But anything which requires further consideration needs to be addressed outside the Confessional; it's not the confessor's responsibility to expect the penitent to engage in a lengthy conversation. What *is* important is to remember

that the Confessional is a boundaried place, and that whatever is spoken of should never be referred to outside of that
space. However, the confessor might suggest that something
be taken to spiritual direction for further consideration.
Conversely, spiritual direction might lead to the suggestion
that the directee consider making their Confession. But many
consider the two ministries best kept separate.

Regular practice of the Ignatian Examen can also help in
identifying what to bring to Confession as well as being a
useful preparation when the vivid awareness of sin may have
faded and Confession seems to have the staleness of a humdrum discipline.

> *If you have the impression that in your prayer you no
> longer need to shed tears for your sins, consider how far
> you have moved away from God, despite the fact that
> you should always be with him. Then you will shed hot
> tears. (Evagrius Ponticus, Chapters on Prayer)*

A Form of Confession is provided in Appendix 3.

Guilt, shame and remorse

Sadly for some, even after making their Confession, a profound sense of guilt and shame can remain and prove a burden.
There's a way in which this is inevitable as our conscience
needs to be informed and adjust to the circumstances of sin.
Most of us can hold a certain sense of remorse about what
we've done without it becoming disabling, but there are those
who will find themselves overburdened by these emotions
and will need help to come to terms with them. Initially, this
is something we can pray about, asking God to show us a
way in which we can make amends and then leaving that
desire in the hands of God. But if we find those emotions
beginning to overwhelm us, we should take that to spiritual

direction, although further help might be needed as one seeks healing for the memory of the weight of sin. Therapy can be sought but, in the end, a person will probably have to learn to carry their burden just as St Paul carried his and accept the 'prick' of conscience (2 Cor. 12.7).

Guilt can also be connected with pride and the difficulty of accepting that we have done something wrong. Although Confession is an important means of healing grace, if someone cannot accept that they are forgiven then this needs to be addressed in spiritual direction. Both guilt and shame can act as real distractions to accepting the grace of God and, in that sense, need to be resisted for they can easily entrap us and carry us deeper into desolation. We may need to carry this burden for some time, but God cannot desire that it should prevent us knowing his love, nor can it please him that we might have a sense that we 'deserve' to carry this burden. So we mustn't give it our active attention, for there's a danger it will swallow us up; rather, we must look to the face of Christ and prayerfully sense his Heart embracing us until the time comes when we, like burdened Christian, can 'lay it all at the foot of the Cross'.

When, through human frailty, the brothers and sisters fail in their high endeavour they will yet return again to Christ with humble contrition and earnest purpose of amendment; and they will hold in special esteem that sacrament of penance and absolution whereby they are cleansed from sin and renewed in the life of grace. (SSF Principles, Day 18)

Questions for reflection

- Read Psalm 139 slowly and reflectively. What is this saying in my heart?
- What irritates me about others? What angers me? What makes me jealous? What might this be telling me about myself?
- When did I last make my Confession? Have I ever made one? What's stopping me? How might I benefit? Who might I approach for help?

Notes

1 Ch. 22, para. 1.
2 *Revelations of Divine Love*, ch. 5, para. 1.
3 Dinah Maria Mulock Craik (1826–87), from *A Life for a Life*, 1859 (reprinted Dodo Press, 2008).
4 John Newton, 'The Imminent Danger and the Only Sure Resource of this Nation', sermon preached at St Mary Woolnoth, London, 28 February 1794.
5 William Palmer, *A Harmony of Anglican Doctrine* (1846), Note XXX.III.
6 Oswald Chambers, 'Continuous Conversion', in *My Utmost for His Highest*, Discovery House, 1935, 28 December.
7 *The Christian Priest Today*, SPCK, 2009 [1972], p. 52.
8 *The Christian Priest Today*, ch. 7: The Priest as Absolver. Those who wish to read further in this matter of hearing Confessions might find help in Martin L. Smith and Julia Gatta, *Go in Peace: The Art of Hearing Confessions*, Morehouse Publishing, 2012.

3

The Heart of a Servant

The diaconate as the wellspring of the priesthood

*Deacons are to proclaim the gospel in word and deed,
as agents of God's purposes of love ... They are to work
with their fellow members in searching out the poor and
weak, the sick and lonely and those who are oppressed
and powerless, reaching into the forgotten corners of
the world, that the love of God may be made visible.
(Ordination of Deacons: The Greeting)*

I was blind but now I see

My own vocation to the sacramental priesthood took many
years to be realized after I first sensed a call in 1966. As the
years rolled on, in spite of attending selection conferences,
I was not recommended for training, and became confused.
Why did I still feel this call if no one else recognized it? Something which, I'm sure, will resonate with others.

One morning, when I was in my early-20s, as I emerged
from Piccadilly underground station my attention was caught
by a young man lying on the pavement asleep on a sheet of
cardboard. I'd seen many like him before, but on this particular day at this particular moment something touched a place
deep in my heart, something shifted as I heard a voice say:
'Why him, not me?' And that question haunted me.

It is not enough to give bread.
Love must be your calling.
Then will the poor forgive us
the bread that we give them.[1]

It's probable that we've all had such epiphanies when the scales fell from our eyes and God spoke in the depth of our soul. Shortly afterwards I shared the experience with my director, who suggested I make a retreat with the Sisters of the Love of God at their skete at Bede House.[2] In that place of solitude and silence, I came across a notice, pinned to the chapel Intercession Board, from a Fr Bill Kirkpatrick asking for volunteers to work among homeless young people at Centrepoint in Soho, London.[3] And God again tugged at my heartstrings. Consequently, I volunteered there in my spare time for about three years and found the ministry deeply rewarding. Fr Bill referred to it as contemplatively 'being there' on the edges of society, reaching out to the 'least of these who are members of my family' (Matt. 25.40). During that time, three Franciscan brothers took up residence and I began joining them in their oratory as often as I could. A growing relish for the rhythm of prayer and service led me, a year later, to give up my job and join the Franciscans – the rest is my story. You'll have yours. But from it all that 'diaconal dialectic' between contemplation and action has remained fundamental, as has the understanding that God most often visits us in the small, seemingly insignificant and unexpected things of life.

Cordial love of the neighbour does not consist in feelings. This love flows not from a heart of flesh but from the heart of our will. (St Jane Frances de Chantal, Foundress of the Visitation Order)

৵

IN THE WORLD BUT NOT OF THE WORLD

Paradigm shifts

The movement into ordained life needs to be understood as a paradigm shift – a life-change of fundamental magnitude the power of which shouldn't be underestimated. From the beginning of training through the years of formation, we will experience such shifts at both conscious and unconscious levels as our 'internal plates' are moved by forces beyond our control. Through it all, we need to exercise patience and allow time and space for the internal processes to work as we begin to assimilate aspects of vocation that will be strange and unfamiliar, often at odds with what we have known. This will take time, often years, and will involve various tensions. For example, those with families will have to face particular demands on time and attention. People may have to move from a regulated life to one with little regulation where the onus is on the individual taking responsibility for what they do. Some will need to adjust to the demands of parish life after having had a secular job and what was a 'nine to five' life becomes a life that can seem to have no boundaries. A person who carried many responsibilities may find they have to face having none, yet, at the same time, will find there are external expectations from clergy and congregations as well as one's own, internal, ones. And that existential question – who am I before God?

Amid the wonders of a new life there will be times of great darkness and doubt. What have I let myself in for? Can I trust God? Have I made a massive mistake? Do I need an 'exit strategy' if it all goes pear-shaped? Help! These and other questions, doubts and fears are inevitable and reveal that there is movement going on. Apart from taking all this to

God in prayer (so important), this is where a good spiritual director can be of great benefit. And don't worry, this state of affairs won't last forever! Have patience with the slow work of God. We're naturally impatient and can forget the importance of this journey, which takes time and will involve periods of instability which accompany change. It's important to embrace and be open to these experiences which, by God's grace working in the soul, are part of the process of realizing one's vocation. Accept the anxiety and uncertainty, and sit lightly to it all. Don't let it overwhelm you, turn your eye upon Jesus and sit prayerfully in that compassionate gaze. Don't give in to desolation or despair – remember, vocation is a costly business involving losing and finding, letting go and discovering; poverty and riches.

'White space'

In all this, the need for 'white space' becomes apparent. Originating in the design industry, the term denotes the space that surrounds the written word. But it's also relevant to spirituality and growth because of the way it expresses the need for areas of nothingness, where life appears as a blank canvas waiting for God to make a mark – times that seem valueless yet enable the undistracted presence of God. It's another term for that poverty of spirit, that desire to abandon all to God, that selling all one has which Jesus told one young man was necessary to discipleship (Luke 18.8ff.).

It's vital that uncluttered space is allowed for the vocational process to be realized, just as a gardener, after planting, needs to leave the soil undisturbed. This may be formal, as in contemplative prayer, quiet days and retreats, or we may suddenly find ourselves with nothing much to do. There's a strong temptation (I know) to fill it 'productively', but that would be to avoid the importance of times of apparent emptiness and nothingness; rather, we need to tell ourselves that it's

OK to slow down, 'do nothing', open a book, listen to music (preferably not noisy …), visit an art gallery, read poetry. Gaze. Such periods are of immense importance, especially in the early stages of living out this new vocation, because they allow the Holy Spirit undistracted opportunities to work within us and for our vocation to 'embed' itself.

It could be said that we need to develop contemplative prayer because of the way it enables 'white space' where the Word may be revealed. This is a vital aspect of diaconal formation for it reminds us of the foundational importance of realising that we are not simply called to be 'ministers of the gospel' but, as Fr. Bill Kirkpatrick expressed it, 'contemplative activists'. The introduction of contemplative looking will guard our compassion from simply emotional activism to reaching out to others from the Heart of God. Of course what emerges in times of contemplation can be disturbing, which is why we need a spiritual director with whom to process what is becoming apparent. However, it may be that only those who gaze *on* that space observe the effects of that revelation – the 'page' itself may be unaware of what's been imprinted. Our task is to make sure that the page is clear and remains 'white', open only for the Word. It is the writer, not the page, who determines what is written.

*White space allows what is written
to become visible to the beholder
though that on which it is visible
may be unaware of what is present.*

As I notice more and more people wandering around with music devices plugged into their ears, I wonder what's getting blocked out? The hills *are* alive with the sound of music but not the kind that comes out of an iPod. Priests, of all people, might experiment with being countercultural and positively *want* to develop white space for God, to waste time with God and seek out places of undistracted encounter and holiness, opening themselves to the gaze of Divine Compassion. Embracing such times of apparent nothingness is an important witness to the reality of God (Eph. 1.3ff.).

Waiting for God

This problem of 'waiting on God' can express itself with a feeling that the diaconate is an unnecessary time in limbo before the 'real work' begins. I've even heard of deacons who are treated as 'second-class citizens'. But it's out of diaconal life that priesthood flourishes! The fact that it's the responsibility of the deacon to proclaim the Gospel at the Eucharist isn't a liturgical nicety but an affirmation that our primary call, however we later express our vocation, is to affirm God's presence in the world, no matter how the world might have become deaf and blind to that presence. The hermit-priest no less than the prison chaplain needs to be aware of the Christ who is in all and fills all. Sadly, some church ministers seem prone to live in their own 'bubble', and I'm sure we all know of clergy – and congregations – who exist as if the rest of the world didn't! The invitation to be 'perfect as your heavenly father is perfect' (Matt. 5.48) is meant to enable the Church's effect on the whole, not to make us only able to connect with like-minded people. The diaconate needs to be a time when we root ourselves in both world and Church.

CALLED TO OBEDIENCE

Sadly, the call to be perfect can easily slip into perfectionism, which, apart from anything else, can lead some clergy to
become pompous, arrogant or domineering; people who've
lost the heart of a servant and forgotten that *their* heart needs
to be filled with humility. For they follow One who exercised
that virtue.

> *Let us touch the dying, the poor, the lonely and the*
> *unwanted according to the graces we have received and*
> *let us not be ashamed or slow to do the humble work.*
> *(St Teresa of Calcutta)*

For many years, I lived under the religious vow of Obedience.
It's not an easy vow, but it is fundamental to Religious Life,
not because it enables autocracy (though it can) but because
it can defeat pride. I was taught that the word 'obedience' is
made from the conflation of two Latin words *ob* and *audio*
which, put together, mean to listen deeply – beneath what
might be said. The obedience of Jesus' mother has always
been understood to have reversed the sin of Eve, and the 'Ave'
of Gabriel is to be mirrored by our own 'Yes' to God, a 'yes'
that needs to be present in diaconal ministry. It's the basis
for that 'spirituality of service', of 'being there', that lies at its
heart. In all this, of course, it's equally important that the one
who commands obedience does not do so in a conceited way
but, knowing themselves what it is like to be under authority,
with care and compassion towards those in their charge.

Pride

This matter of defeating pride and bending and softening a strong will is of great importance. As the SSF Principles say: 'The brothers and sisters desire ... to surrender their wills to the will of God, in the spirit of perfect obedience, that being delivered from self-will and pride they may find true freedom and peace and be ready instruments which he can use for his purposes' (Day 10). Pride has been recognized as the greatest sin, which is why the importance of humility in the lives of those seeking to live more closely to Christ has long been realized. 'Take my yoke upon you, and learn from me; for I am gentle and humble in heart, and you will find rest for your souls' (Matt. 11.29). Of course, we all need a certain sense of pleasure and satisfaction in our abilities and achievements, but pride can turn into a dangerous master if not controlled by humility.

ॐ

CALLED TO HUMILITY

I guess many who emerge from training think they 'know it all' (I did), yet we must never stop learning, and often in surprising ways. For us, learning also involves opening the ear of our heart to listen to what God might be saying through others – and having the humility to listen to how others perceive us. I found it very hard, but in the end so rewarding, to have to listen to how my Franciscan brothers perceived me – how they recognized elements of arrogance, the inability to really listen and so on, insights that were painful and sometimes had to be said with some force to get through my defences but which, in the end, helped me to recognize myself. To know myself. 'The most powerful weapon against the devil is humility', taught St Vincent de Paul, 'for as he does not know at all how to employ it, neither does he know how to defend himself against it'.[4]

Humility is the foundation of any genuine spirituality for it concerns the ground of our being. It doesn't mean feeling wretched about ourselves but realizing the truth of who we are in the eyes of God; that we are dust, but dust destined for glory (Eph. 3.14ff.). The 'Principles' of the Spiritual Association of the Compassionate Hearts of Jesus and Mary (CHJM) declare humility to be: 'the ground of our being, the recognition of the truth about God and ourselves; the awareness of our own insufficiency and dependence, seeing that we have nothing which we have not received. As St John Chrysostom said, "Humility is the root, mother, nurse, foundation, and bond of all virtue"' (Day 24).[5] Just as God's humility brought about the Incarnation so those who are his servants need to remember that they walk the same path. Many have noted that although there's no shortage of clergy wanting to serve in flourishing churches, fewer ask to be sent to poorer, marginalized places. The heroic example of those nineteenth-century priests who served in the slums of our towns and cities has left a lasting legacy, which is still lauded. Yet how many want to live in some of our neglected housing estates? Just as Jesus laid aside the splendour of his divinity and took an outward form that was often despised and rejected, so we are invited to consider making a 'preferential option for the poor'.[6] In the same way that a priest, on Maundy Thursday, imitates the example of Christ by washing – and kissing – the feet of those they serve, so we are to venerate him in those whom society can easily ignore. Perhaps we might consider how our spirituality helps us become priests of the Magnificat: 'He has brought down the powerful from their thrones, and lifted up the lowly' (Luke 1.52). Doesn't the fact that God chose to be incarnated in a small, remote and poor village have something to tell us about our choices?

ॐ

CALLED TO BE A SERVANT

My vows to the Lord I will fulfil
before all His people.
A thanksgiving sacrifice I make:
I will call on the Lord's name.
(Psalm 116.15f.)

The servant, under orders from a higher authority (Matt.
8.5ff.), has to a great extent lost their autonomy, their ability
to control things, and this can be costly and challenging to the
newly ordained. Three of the most important developments
in my own life as a Religious came about as a consequence
of obedience, but on each occasion I accepted them grudgingly. All involved crisis but, as the word suggests, proved
to be fundamental turning points in my life and vocation. As
I struggled with what was being asked of me, I had to face
my own sense of inadequacy and fear, not least of failure;
my sense of pride; my certainty that I was right and misunderstood, etc. Yet, on each occasion, as I was stretched
out of my 'comfort-zone', I began to grow in ways I could
never have imagined if I'd decided what I wanted to do and,
consequently, my life was enriched, and I came to realize the
truth that 'My grace is sufficient for you, for power is made
perfect in weakness' (2 Cor. 12.9). So we need to recognize
something of the beauty of service, a beauty rooted in Christ,
and discover a joy in realizing him as the one who inspires
our life whom we long to share with others.

All things are possible to him who believes, they are less
difficult to him who hopes, they are more easy to him
who loves, and still more easy to him who perseveres in
the practice of these three virtues. (Br Lawrence of the
Resurrection 1614–91)

The beauty of service

It may be countercultural, but there's something glorious about one who serves. I recall being among a vast throng of pilgrims attending the Feast of the Dormition of Mary at the Coptic Orthodox monastery near Bayad, south of Cairo. Among them was a young man selling Coke. He was clearly educated, so I asked him why he was 'just selling Coke'. 'I do it for Jesus,' was his humbling reply. And that simple reply reminded me how we always need to recall that the gift of the priesthood is given to the deacon: it is from that ground that priesthood flourishes. Although no longer required, some priests and deacons still wear the maniple, placed over the left arm at the Eucharist, as a reminder of the call to be the servant of the servants of God.

> May I deserve, O Lord, to bear the maniple of weeping and sorrow in order that I may joyfully reap the reward of my labours. (Prayer said when placing the maniple over the left arm)

One Anglican bishop made a practice of refusing to ordain anyone to the priesthood until they could demonstrate they had got to grips with diaconate. 'I thought it far too dangerous', he said, 'to offer them the "power" of priestly ordination otherwise.' He tells the story of an occasion when a very evangelical bishop went to preside at Mass in an Anglo-Catholic church in Texas. In the sacristy a young priest was vesting. The bishop looked at him in amazement and asked, 'Where's your maniple?' 'We don't wear it because it gets in the way at the altar,' replied the priest. The bishop asked him if he knew that the maniple represented the servanthood of the deacon. 'Yes,' he responded. 'Then if you're gonna wear those fancy duds, wear them all and *always* let the deaconate "get in the way" of your priesthood.'[7]

The Practice of the Presence of God

With that servant's heart the deacon recalls that it is Christ they serve. Jesus' parable of the Judgement of the Nations (Matt. 25.31–40) is a stark yet beautiful statement of faith and, maybe, should be the one read at the ordination of deacons. It's certainly one we need to meditate on. Often. There's a poem by the great Sufi poet, Rumi, which I've always valued:

> *This being human is a guest house.*
> *Every morning a new arrival.*
> *A joy, a depression, meanness,*
> *some momentary awareness comes*
> *as an unexpected visitor.*
> *Welcome and entertain them all.*
> *Even if they're a crowd of sorrows*
> *who violently sweep your house*
> *empty of its furniture.*
> *Still treat each guest honourably.*
> *He may be clearing you out for some new delight.*
> *The dark thought, the shame, the malice,*
> *meet them at the door laughing,*
> *and invite them in.*[8]

The poem brings to mind the spirituality of Br Lawrence of the Resurrection whose book, *The Practice of the Presence of God*, is still a bestseller. Lawrence, a lay brother in one of the Carmelite communities in Paris, described himself as 'a doorkeeper in the house of God', and his life has much to teach about the diaconal role. In his fourth 'conversation', for example, he wrote: 'We ought not to be weary of doing little things for the love of God, who regards not the greatness of the work, but the love with which it is performed.'

Yet even our service can occasion abuse, as many who

work in our public services know, so we should never be surprised when we're insulted or attacked for what we do. St Teresa of Calcutta, who believed in offering 'something beautiful for God', is reputed to have pinned a version of this meditation on her wall:

> *People are often unreasonable, illogical and self-centred; Forgive them anyway. If you are kind, people may accuse you of selfish, ulterior motives; Be kind anyway. If you are honest and frank, people may cheat you; be honest and frank anyway. What you spend years building, someone could destroy overnight; build anyway. The good you do today, people will often forget tomorrow; do good anyway. Give the world the best you have, and it may never be enough; give the world the best you've got anyway. You see, in the final analysis, it is between you and your God. It was never between you and them anyway.*[9]

So the diaconal ministry is not to be thought of as *merely* a necessary interlude before the 'real' ministry begins but as a time for nurturing the heart of a servant and to firmly establish the consciousness that 'I have come among you as one who serves' (Luke 22.27).

'*My diaconate will be the heart-wood of my priesthood.*'[10]

CALLED TO BE A PROPHET

Whether, then, we minister in a parish, monastery, chaplaincy or wherever, we need to keep an eye on the world we're called to serve and where we're to be salt and light; we are partners in that process of conversion that heralds the Reign of God.

Herald of the Great King

In his *First Life of St Francis*, Thomas of Celano tells us that one of the key moments in the process of Francis realizing his own vocation occurred when, after beginning his life of poverty, he was accosted by robbers as he walked through the woods near Assisi. When they demanded to know who he was, he replied that he was a 'herald of the Great King'. Considering his ragged clothes, they decided he was being sarcastic and proceeded to beat him up and push him into a ditch. When they'd gone away, Celano says that Francis climbed out and, with great joy, began to sing the praises of God. Hopefully a deacon won't get beaten up as they go about their ministry, but I find the idea of the deacon as a 'herald of a Great King' enormously exciting, not least because it is their responsibility to proclaim the Gospel at the Eucharist.

The thought that deacons share in Christ's prophetic calling and our need to give particular expression to that has always been a bit of a challenge for me. I also recognize that the gospel, which cuts sharper than any two-edged sword, will mean that some experience God calling them to particular actions arising from the social context. Diaconal life is the fertile ground from which prophetic activity emerges as we daily abandon ourselves into the hands of God. This is what we are called to do as we seek to fulfil God's will and become re-formed into the likeness of Christ. That *conversatio morum* of which St Benedict speaks applies to the heart of the world as much as to the individual: but it all begins with me.

Happy the man who considers the poor and the weak.
The Lord will save him in the day of evil,
will guard him, give him life, make him happy in the land
and will not give him up to the will of his foes.
(Psalm 41.1f.)

Apart, then, from the ministry of servanthood, the deacon is the one who is called to stand in that midway point between the Church and the world with an eye on both, a 'boundary-crosser' who descends from the sanctuary into the people to proclaim the gospel. The primary call of the deacon is to proclaim the Word of God and reveal that Good News to the world in word and deed: 'Whoever serves me must follow me, and where I am, there will my servant be also. Whoever serves me, the Father will honour' (John 12.26).

Those who would claim to be His servants and follow Him must be diligent in ministry to others. (Luke 4.18), (Isa 61.1) Compassion impels us to work to alleviate suffering; to dethrone ourselves from the centre of our world and put Another there; to honour the sanctity of every single human being, treating everybody, without exception, with absolute justice, equity and respect. Companions will reject all that demeans others and find ways of working for the common good. (CHJM Principles, Day 27)

Questions for reflection

- How can I develop a sense of serving Christ as I seek to serve others?
- What might be a right and wrong sense of 'pride' in the context of ministry?
- How can I develop a more compassionate heart?
- In what ways am I being a 'herald of the Great King'?

Notes

1 Lyric by the American composer James Primosch based on a line from the film *Monsieur Vincent*.

2 A *skete* is a collection of hermitages. Individual members of the *skete* join together for common worship. They developed at a time when monks were in need of the protection that living together gave.

3 Father Bill was director of Centrepoint in Soho, a project founded by Fr Ken Leech to help young homeless people.

4 Anonymous, *A Year with the Saints*, 1891, p. 47.

5 Their 'Principles' are based, in part, on those of SSF. The quote from St John Chrysostom comes from his *Commentary on the Acts of the Apostles*.

6 Pope Francis, *Evangelii Gaudium*, 2013, para. 199.

7 Quoted to the author in correspondence with Bishop Laurie Green.

8 *Rumi: Selected Poems*, trans. Coleman Barks, Penguin Books, 2004.

9 Based on 'The Paradoxical Commandments' printed with permission of the author © Kent M. Keith, 1968, renewed 2001.

10 Susan Sayers, quoted by Bishop Laurie Green in correspondence with the author.

4

Formed in the Likeness of Christ

Formators and formation

God calls his people to follow Christ, and forms us into a royal priesthood, a holy nation, to declare the wonderful deeds of him who has called us out of darkness into his marvellous light. (Ordination of Deacons: The Greeting)

The Lord is my light and my help;
whom shall I fear?
The Lord is the stronghold of my life;
whom should I dread?
(Psalm 27.1)

Christ's oblation and our formation

I realize that formation through training and Initial Ministerial Education (IME) is addressed in many different documents. What's written here isn't meant to duplicate that but to address some of the issues that have arisen as I've listened to those recently ordained. It also seeks to focus on the fact that behind all ministerial formation is the call to a life of holiness, because I sense that sometimes that gets forgotten. For just as Christ loved the Church and gave himself to make us holy, so her ministers, in a special way, share in that calling – to a life of faith, hope and love (1 Cor. 13.13) because these virtues are the bedrock of our calling. But I wonder if, in reality, training does that? And if not, why not? These days we may not speak much about Christ's 'oblation' to the Father, but priests are called to holiness by making their lives an offering to God.

This chapter also concerns the role of 'formators',[1] and while the word's a bit inelegant it does remind us that clergy are not just to be trained, they're also – and more importantly – to be *formed* in the likeness of Christ, as noted by Diocesan guides. This must be the foundational principle for those given the specific honour of living out of the priesthood of Christ who invites us to share all things with him (Matt. 11.28f.): 'He must increase and I must decrease' (John 3.30).

I am the vine, you are the branches. Those who abide in me and I in them bear much fruit because apart from me you can do nothing. (John 15.5)

I'm sure those responsible for priestly formation will be aware of the importance of the example they're setting, so my first thought concerns what our activity and commitment to prayer and its rhythm say about the priesthood. How far are we aware of, and not at the mercy of, our fears and desires, compulsions and memories and all those other hidden movements which can determine how we live out our calling? Working with another is not always easy, and generosity is needed in our dealings. Sadly, I've listened to stories of clergy who work together but don't relate, where one avoids having any meaningful relationship with the other or assistant priests are not treated as mature adults. Some even experience abusive behaviour, a matter that needs to be dealt with in appropriate ways. At times, it's clear that shared prayer has become a formality or the Office is not prayed daily, and while there may be particular reasons why the latter is difficult – and those who are also in secular employment may need to develop a different pattern – what are we saying if daily prayer is not experienced as essential?

FORMATIONAL SUPERVISION

The importance of proper *ongoing* supervision (and reflective practice) is recognized by the Church of England. My own experience of supervising those in formation began when I was a Novice Guardian and responsible, under the Provincial Minister, for those who entered SSF in the UK. I wish I'd known then what I know now! Since then, I've joined the Association for Pastoral Supervision and Education (APSE), which was founded in 2005 to promote good practice in that field in the UK, and it's from a background of supervising clergy that I offer the following, which seeks to highlight some aspects of this ministry.

First, and this may be obvious, supervision must be about more than just the nuts and bolts of daily ministry; it must also concern the hidden, overlooked processes connected with ministry. 'The unexamined life', said Socrates, 'is not worth living',[2] and clergy, in particular, need to live reflective lives. One of the most useful tools in this regard is the Examen mentioned earlier, a practice which many find of enormous help.

The Examen

Ignatius's great gift to the Church, a simple version of which is provided in Appendix 4, concerns how we can notice the movements of God within the soul and how we respond to those movements. Its focus is not on me, it is on *God in me*; it's not about how well or how poorly I do but about how I respond to God's loving me. Its goal is to develop a heart with a discerning vision to find God in all things. It helps us become more aware of our inner movements – the feelings, motives and inspirations – that deepen and direct our lives to, or pull us away from, God. It helps us to notice where we've hardened our heart. Looking at these movements makes us more attuned to the inspirations of the Holy Spirit and more alert to the promptings of what Ignatius called the 'evil spirit'.

While there are many suggested ways of practising the Examen, the best thing is to experiment until you find a way that's most helpful and natural for you. It can be done once or twice a day, once every few days, once a week … in fact however often a person feels moved to do it with the greatest benefit. Many use it as a preparation for keeping a reflective journal, which they use in spiritual direction or pastoral supervision. The more you practise it, the more natural it becomes until it becomes a way of consciousness, of being in ever closer relationship with God. What's important is to begin the process of reflective living.

Learning agreements

While the importance of these is recognized and addressed in various ways, some have noted that they would value revisiting them from time to time to make sure they are adequate. At times there can be confusion about expectations, and this will need to be addressed in supervision which needs to look at the *person* beneath the role and the processes that are helping or hindering them.

Basic norms of supervision

The practice of 'noticing' is fundamental to both reflective living and supervision, and it's as important, when supervising others, not only to attend to what's happening to the other but also what is happening within oneself *as* one listens.[3]

In St John's account of the Resurrection he describes how Mary, Peter and John experienced the event (20.1–10). In relation to their encounters, most English translations use the word 'see' in place of the Greek for 'notice', 'wonder' and 'perceive', words indicating a deepening process. In a similar way, supervisors need to notice and wonder about what is happening in them and the supervisee as an account unfolds. A number of simple insights can be helpful.

One concerns the need not to get bogged down in the content of what's being said. Rather, where's the feeling – the need – the weight? Sit lightly to the facts and notice where one is moved. Don't just address the presenting problem, but notice where the emphasis lies or greatest feeling is expressed in what's being said. What's trying to emerge beneath the narrative? Reflecting back what's been noticed and wondering about the greatest need, struggle or feeling that's perceived. Does that need sharing? Where might God be working in all this? Has an image arisen – an echo from Scripture – that needs to be shared? Remember, supervision isn't just about problem-solving or training; it concerns a deepening of awareness of what prevents us responding from a place of freedom. While most dioceses and churches offer a wide range of courses and events connected with developmental skills, formation must go further than this. One diocese recognizes this and says its programme of IME: 'intends to enable curates to mature in ministerial character, being *formed into the likeness of Christ* for the service of God's people'.[4]

Formators and formation

The role of the Training Incumbent (TI) *can* be felt as yet another responsibility laid on their shoulders, and some, I know, feel that they no longer have time for their own spiritual direction – or supervision. Yet it's at just such times that the priest needs these two ministries more than ever.

'Successful' clergy also need to listen to any nagging, inner voice warning them that while all might seem well, 'success' might actually be putting them in danger. This should alert them to watch for difficulties which may emerge between them and their curate(s).

There can also be problems over trust, and it's important to build a healthy relationship (social and spiritual). Some curates wonder how much they can reveal about themselves and whether their TI will *really* listen to them non-judgementally, which is why curates need a spiritual director who can listen to them in this way as things begin to surface in the early stages of ordained life. Formators need to listen to the needs they become aware of in obvious or hidden ways and will, themselves, have a need for proper supervision of their ministry. What expectations does the formator have of those in their care and when are these addressed? The person is, hopefully, doing their best and will need affirmation, one of the 'Five Tasks of Supervision', which is to be:

1 Affirmative: encouraging and supportive.
2 Formative: enabling of growth through theory, sharing knowledge and insights;
3 Normative: monitoring of good practice.
4 Restorative: a safe place where feelings can be discharged.
5 Contemplative: fostering a contemplative attitude through a deeper awareness of God's presence.

While there are many ways of understanding the 'task' of pastoral supervision, the above would seem to be basic but, sadly, is not always being offered. Because clashes and mis-understandings can easily develop, it's important for those working together to develop ways of learning to respect and value each other. I recall a time when I was a Franciscan, and a number of us took part in one of the first Myers-Briggs Personality Type Indicator (MBTI) programmes in the UK, at the end of which we realized the 'who, what and why' of how we related. 'So that's why I find you so difficult!' was the oft-repeated cry as we learnt to respect our differences. But where problems continue, it's appropriate to refer the matter to one's own supervisor or the appropriate pastoral authority. In the end, both those exercising authority and those who work with them need to remember they are servants of Christ.

∾

TRANSFORMED INTO THE LIKENESS OF CHRIST

As a Franciscan, one of the things I was grateful for was the way our Principles stressed the need to live a balanced life rooted in Christ, for ministry was but an aspect of our calling. Behind ministry we were to be rooted in and live out of that core-self which primarily sought, and desired to be found by, God. In a similar way, the primary calling of priests is into this same dynamic relationship with God in Christ from where our vocation springs. For while we are part of the Body of Christ, our 'ministry is not an extension of the common Christian priesthood *but belongs to another realm of the gifts of the Spirit*.[5] Thus the section on 'Prayer' in the SSF Principles begins by saying: 'Praise and prayer constitute the atmosphere in which we must strive to live. We must endeavour to maintain a constant recollection of the presence of God and of the unseen world. An ever-deepening devotion to Christ is the hidden source of all our strength and joy' (Day 14).

Immersion in Christ through prayer and Scripture was foundational. I say that because even for a religious, prayer and feeding deeply on Scripture through, for example, *Lectio Divina*[6] can easily get squeezed out. So another of the Principles reminded us that: '(Brothers and sisters) must always be on their guard against the constant temptation to let other work encroach upon the hours of prayer, remembering that if they seek in this way to increase the bulk of their activity it can only be at the cost of its true quality and value' (Day 16). If 'Christ is the pattern of their calling', as the bishop says at the beginning of the liturgy for the Ordination of Deacons, we should notice how frequently Jesus withdrew from public ministry. While this has long been recognized as important by many in the Church, others, like Richard Foster and Eugene Peterson, are now beginning to understand the value of contemplative prayer, solitude and silence in Christian discipleship. But are those in formation encouraged to develop the practice of finding a 'place apart'? Does their Training Incumbent set a good example by taking Quiet Days and Retreats? What does their example say?

Secret ways to successful ministry

Are we, in an age of increasing noise and restlessness, falling for the temptation to offer lots of activities hoping that this will attract people? No wonder some clergy get exhausted by having to create services each week – and then 'put them on'. There's no shortage of websites (often connected with megachurches) devoted to how to develop a 'successful' ministry. Although we must not ignore the need for churches to grow, many sense there's a danger in the notion of success in relation to the Church, and some programmes for evangelism can begin to feel akin to growing a business. Having worked in insurance sales, I recognize some of the telltale signs of the overlap between successful selling and church growth. It often means that prayer, in these situations, becomes about asking God to do things – make things happen – as *we* want it rather than developing a heart open *to* God.

> *I do not pray for success, I ask for faithfulness.*
> *(St Teresa of Calcutta)*

I wonder if you, like so many others, crave silence or whether your life is so full of noise and restlessness that you fear facing what might become present in silence? I always recall running a school Quiet Day and inviting a group of 14-year-olds to experience a minute of silence. 'How was that?' I asked at the end. 'Boring', said one, which led me to suggest that he might consider why being with himself for a minute might be boring! Thankfully these days young people are being introduced to practices of Mindfulness in schools – and some church schools are turning to the great Christian traditions of silence and meditation to help children realize the rich traditions and disciplines that we have at our disposal in order to put them in touch with their inner Self and the Other. But I wonder if we, ministers of the gospel, are being formed and are helping others to be formed in the great traditions of Christian prayer? Or are we ignoring our heritage? What *we* have to offer is a path to encountering God: we're not just to be good at 'bringing people in' but in enabling them, when they *are* in, to deepen their relationship with God. Thankfully, some involved in the Church Growth Movement recognize that a healthy church is one which is living out of the Beatitudes rather than simply increasing in numbers.

A *career in the Church*

And then there's a sense that some see the Church offering them a career path, a way to success. Jobs advertised in religious newspapers can appeal to this feeling of wanting to climb the ladder. How many of us want to accept a 'failing' church as the young Curé did who was sent by his bishop to that poor village of Ars? Too often, one comes across clergy who have begun to feel overlooked in the 'preferment stakes'. While it's understandable that we want to be recognized for the good we've accomplished, we must also beware this turning into a desire to be offered more 'successful' positions. The life of Fr

Stanton, the great Anglo-Catholic priest who died in 1913, is a moving example of the value of a hidden ministry. Priested at the age of 25, his entire ministry – almost 50 years – was spent as a curate at St Alban's, Holborn, yet when he died thousands lined the route of his funeral procession. One of the many insights he is reputed to have shared with some Oxford ordinands was simply: 'When you're priests, teach your people to love the Lord Jesus. Don't teach them to be C of E. Teach them to love the Lord Jesus.' As the Revd E. F. Russell preached at St Alban's on the Sunday after his death: 'He found Christ and loved Christ in the souls of men, and … most of all in the least worthy; for this was one of the marked features of his love that, like his Master, he loved the lost sheep and the publicans and the sinners … and this brought him often into friendly relations with persons and creeds and strange varieties of beliefs or unbeliefs, which at times were misunderstood.' It can be hard to feel overlooked in the pre-ferment stakes, but we follow a Master who wasn't interested in developing a career but of being faithful to his Father. This is what all the great priests of the past remind us.

I realize that clergy shouldn't be formed for failure, but are ordinands being trained to face the probability that at some point they'll have to face the end of hopes and dreams, cherished plans or projects into which they've sunk time and effort? Many Religious Orders, facing declining numbers and their possible disappearance, grasp this situation as an opportunity for growth in faith in the Paschal Mystery. For we follow one who was a failure in the sight of most of his contemporaries, yet who could never have been a failure in the sight of his Father: Jesus wasn't formed for success but for faithfulness (Rev. 1.5; 3.14).

Formed for heaven

So the First Principle and Foundation of the *Spiritual Exercises* remind us that 'God's purpose in creating us is to draw forth from us a response of love and service here on earth ... that we may attain our goal of everlasting happiness with him in heaven.'[7] Yet what we're often formed for is not this, but a role. Of course, we *have* ministries, ministries that are Christ's in which he invites us to share. But we should not forget what he said to his disciples after they had experienced some success in their mission and ministry: 'Nevertheless, do not rejoice in this, that the spirits submit to you, but rejoice that your names are written in heaven' (Luke 10.20).

So we're not to get attached to results, people liking us, our abilities, etc. In a culture where success is everything, let's not forget that our faith is countercultural; Christianity isn't about success but about failure being redeemed. Popularity, growing congregations, people speaking highly of us and so on are full of their own dangers; they may be a cause of thanksgiving but, if given the wrong kind of attention, can lead us down the road to nowhere (Deut. 8.10–20). What matters is that our names are written in heaven, that our 'core-self' is rooted in the knowledge that we are God's loved and precious child. We're to be 'doorkeepers of Heaven',[8] men and women whose primary call is to enable others to encounter holiness, to encounter God. And that encounter has an evangelizing ability. One need only recall the appeal of holy places, the attraction of plainsong and other sacred music, of mystical art or monastic liturgies to recognize that the desire for God is still present in human beings even if they're not attracted by what goes on in our churches. Priests are to be formed as 'encouragers of faith' in an age of carelessness. We're to invite people to notice the doorway to the Divine, which may not be in a church but can often be in the presence of nature or art, which, bearing the imprint of the Creator, offers such an opening. We're to incarnate the holiness of God as we seek to respond to the call to become instruments of his reign (Matt. 6.9f.) and given to that *conversatio morum* (conversion of the heart) which reflects our desire for him (Ps. 27).

Formed for compassion

Let the final word in this chapter be spoken by Pope Francis. In his *Evangelii Gaudium*, he wrote of the way Jesus 'summoned us to a *revolution of tenderness*' towards others and towards ourselves.[9] We're to be formed as expressions – sacraments – of this desire, to be full of faith and hope in an unbelieving world; to be constantly converted to compassion and tenderness; to be priests of the Heart of Jesus. What a glorious calling! And it's in prayer we experience our need for, and capacity for, this great gift of tenderness which begins in the heart but is expressed in our lives.

> *With a tenderness which never disappoints, but is always capable of restoring our joy, (God) makes it possible for us to lift up our heads and to start anew. Let us not flee from the resurrection of Jesus.*[10]

Questions for reflection

- If someone were to observe your day, what would they learn about the priestly life? How do you feel about that? What might need changing to pattern it after Christ?
- In what ways does supervision/spiritual direction help an ordained person?
- If you are a formator, what image might you have of yourself in that role: Midwife? Sculptor? Teacher? Is there any aspect that needs more attention? Where are you receiving the necessary supervision for this ministry?

Notes

1 'Formation criteria' for clergy in the Church of England were published by the House of Bishops in May 2014.

2 Socrates at his trial in 399 BC.

3 See W. A. Barry and W. J. Connelly, *The Practice of Spiritual Direction*, Bravo Ltd, 2009, p. 65.

4 *Southwark Diocese IME Handbook, 2017–2018.*

5 ARCIC Agreed Statement on Ministry and Ordination II.13. Italics mine.

6 *Lectio divina* is a form of praying with Scripture. See Chapter 6.

7 David L. Fleming SJ, *A Contemporary Reading of the Spiritual Exercises*, Institute of Jesuit Sources, 1980.

8 George Herbert, *Priest to the Temple*, ch. XXIX, cf. Psalm 84.9.

9 Pope Francis, *Evangelii Gaudium*, 2013, para. 88.

10 *Evangelii Gaudium*, para. 3.

5

The Land of Spices

Prayer beyond the beginnings

O OCEAN of Love,
stillness profound
Light of life of all who come to Thee,
Draw me into Thy still peace,
that all the noise of things be stilled
and the music of the soul be all one Note,
Thyself alone, My Lord, my All.[1]

Prayer

The title of this chapter comes from George Herbert's poem, 'Prayer I'. Herbert was a post-Reformation priest, Welshman and metaphysical poet who spent his entire ministry in the small hamlet of Lower Bemerton in Wiltshire. He described prayer as:

> *God's breath in man returning to his birth,*
> *The soul in paraphrase, heart in pilgrimage, ...*
> *The land of spices; something understood.*

Prayer has many definitions – an act of pure love (cf. Eph. 3.14ff.), the desire that all might be enfolded in Christ, the attention we give to the work of the Spirit or the expression of the soul's deepest longings. St John Damascene described it as 'a raising of one's mind and heart to God'.[2] It's as varied as the one who prays and, while having some well-known characteristics and expressions, is but one aspect of Christian spirituality. Yet, for many, prayer is an unrealized adventure. It's sad to encounter young people who are considering how God might be calling them but who've never been taught anything about prayer other than it's about asking God to help those in need or thanking God for things, as important as both those are. Many have never been taught how they might find nourishment through meditative reading of the Scriptures and know nothing of the great traditions of Christian contemplation – a consequence, possibly, of the way some clergy give prayer less attention than they might. Recently a spiritual director told me that:

> *Yet another diocesan bishop said to me last week, 'My priests tell me they don't have time for prayer.' For me all vocation, but particularly all priestly vocation must start with prayer. How can we expect to be 'present' at the Eucharist, with others at their time of greatest need or to be awake to the scriptures without prayer? How can we protect ourselves from the temptations specific to the priestly office without prayer? How can we do anything without that growing comprehension of our need for God's grace that comes through prayer?*

This chapter seeks to address that concern.

࿐

PRIESTLY PRAYER

On my ordination to the priesthood I was given a small, black, leather-bound book entitled *Priestly Prayers*, one of a series published by Burns and Oates in the 1960s. It contained devotions from various sources down the centuries, including a prayer 'For Fellow Priests' from the seventh-century *Missale Mixtum*, which contained the petition:

> *Grant that priests may live in close brotherly union; give them purity of soul and body and guide them into the way of thy will. So by this generously granted grace, we may, through our fraternal charity, be close friends with thee.*

On re-reading it, I immediately conjured up memories of Clergy Houses of old where Father had no more than a bed, gas fire, desk and leather armchair, was surrounded by his (of course) curates and soutanes were always worn. It now seems part of a spirituality of priesthood from another age, an age of hierarchy where the world was neatly divided, everyone knew their place and priests were the third sex. What passed as 'priestly prayer' seemed written for an unmarried male ordained into a caste. So how might we realize 'priestly prayer' today?

Our image of God determines our prayer

It hardly needs saying that our image of God will determine our prayer. In his book *God of Surprises*, Gerry Hughes SJ writes of the way many were taught about 'Good Old Uncle George' – that loving, powerful family relative who is interested in us but is quite demanding and, when visited in his large mansion, turns out to be something of an ogre. I know it's a rather simplistic story, but the question behind it is always the same: what image of God do I have that draws my prayerful response?

I was fortunate in being adopted as a baby for, as I was once reminded, I was a 'chosen' child and had the good fortune to be brought up in a loving and secure family environment. Some of us may not have been so lucky, and a few will have experienced neglect or abuse, whether sexual or emotional, in their upbringing. Those early experiences will shape, to a greater or lesser extent, our sense of God. Can we really trust God? Am I really loved? Do I need to earn that love? All that, and more, will inform our relationship with God and how we exercise parenthood, familial or spiritual. Each of us, especially those who are called to the priesthood, needs to attend to the foundations of our faith and develop the knowledge that we are loved and precious to God, a love that does not need to be earned nor is it conditional. That God looks upon us with compassionate love.

> *O Love that wilt not let me go,*
> *I rest my weary soul in thee;*
> *I give thee back the life I owe,*
> *That in thine ocean depths its flow*
> *May richer, fuller be.*
> *(George Matheson)*

It is that love that lies at the heart of prayer (1 John 4.7f.) – God's loving desire for union with us seeking to draw out a similar desire in us: 'O God, you search me and you know me' (Ps. 139.1). Prayer, St Paul reminds us, is less about what we do for God and more about what we want God to do – and what *God* wants to do – in us (Rom. 8.26f.). Our task in prayer is to co-operate with the Spirit and not impede her workings, which moved St Augustine of Hippo to exclaim: 'You have made us for yourself, O Lord, and our hearts are restless till they find their rest in you.'[3]

Varieties of prayer: imaginative

The unknown writer of the classic medieval work of English spirituality, *The Cloud of Unknowing*, wrote of prayer as a desire to 'pierce the thick cloud of unknowing with the fiery dart of longing love'.[4] Yet most people (inside as well as outside the Church) would, if asked, probably say that prayer is about asking God for things or telling God things. While that is part of prayer, its essence concerns our desire for God.

Although there are many forms of prayer, some of the most helpful make use of the Scriptures to enable an encounter with God in Christ. This is the basis of both Benedictine *Lectio Divina* and Ignatian *Imaginative Prayer*, both of which have been so influential. (John Wesley was accused of being a disciple of the latter[5] and certainly valued Thomas á Kempis' *The Imitation of Christ* and Francis de Sales' *Introduction to the Devout Life*.) Although imaginative prayer is not for everyone, it's a form of prayer that utilizes a faculty we're using all the time. When I was living in the Society of the Sacred Mission (SSM) priory in a poor part of Nottingham in the 1960s, one elderly, poor, devout and half-blind parishioner, Lily Eaton, explained to me that while she couldn't afford to go on holiday she used to ask travel agents for brochures and then imagine visiting the places illustrated: 'I've travelled the world from my armchair – I can imagine the sights – and smell them!' she told me.

Although she didn't know it, in using her senses Lily was exercising that faculty of imagination which is the basis of Ignatian prayer, an approach you might know. One begins by getting rid of distractions and creating an inner space where the word of the Word can speak into our imagination and then slowly reading, or listening to, a text of Scripture (e.g. Luke 5.1–11). Afterwards, using the five senses, exploring the scene:

What do you hear? (birds, water, crowd, Jesus ...)
What do you touch? (oars, ropes, rocking boats ...)
What do you smell? (water, fishing smells, wood ...)
What do you see? (sunshine, water, Jesus, boat, crowds ...)
Was there anything to taste?

Then notice the people inhabiting the scene and your presence among them. Do any stand out? Are you drawn to any?
What do you notice about Jesus? Listen to his words. Who is
he addressing? Is he speaking to you? Looking at you? How
do you feel? Let the scene play out, and if that moves you
beyond the scriptural account, fine. Just keep your eyes fixed
on Jesus. Is there a conversation you want to have with him?
Let that play out, too. Then, as your time of prayer comes
to an end, spend a few minutes noticing what fruit you may
have gained from this experience. Rest with that and ask Jesus
what you should learn from this. End with the Our Father.

Paying attention

So much about prayer concerns paying attention in ever-
deepening ways. Another elderly person who has much to teach
us is the old farmer whom St Jean-Baptiste-Marie Vianney
would regularly find sitting silently in front of the tabernacle
in his church and who, when asked why he did so, simply
replied: 'I looks at him and he looks at me.' This approach,
traditionally called the 'Prayer of Loving Regard',[6] underlies
the Hindu and Buddhist practice known as Dhyana: focusing
and meditating on a point with the intention of becoming
aware of what lies within – knowing the truth about it. It's also
the basis of the 'prayer of loving attention' to the presence of
God in all things, something that was taught by Br Lawrence
and is the subject of *The Cloud of Unknowing* and which,
more recently, people like John Main and Thomas Keating
have popularized through their teaching of *Centring Prayer*.
It's a form of prayer that can be utilized as you walk through
your parish or wherever you work: take it slowly, notice your
breathing, pay attention to everything you see and embrace
it with love. Use your senses one at a time to connect you to
the place where you are – see it, smell it, touch it ... Don't
let yourself be distracted. And give thanks to God for it. The

most recent term to describe all this is, of course, mindfulness. I often suggest to clergy who say they haven't time to pray that they try walking down the street with attentive awareness or sit in their office and give attention to those around them. Notice everything with your eye of compassion. Try not to let six different things play around in your head; they will want to, but you don't need to encourage them. Take time to notice the wonders on your doorstep and don't keep up a running commentary on it all; wonder at it rather than judge it. Be present to it. This is the kind of prayer that can happen anywhere. Those who lead busy lives and may not have much opportunity to find a quiet church to pray in can use it when driving the car, travelling on a train, working out in the gym, etc. rather than giving attention to what they might find on their mobile phone or iPad.

> *It is not necessary to have great things to do. I turn my little omelette in the pan for the love of God.*[7]

This matter of seeing and hearing was a constant matter to which Jesus gave attention as the beloved disciple recounts in his Gospel. So it's a great pity that some clergy reject the need for contemplative prayer, consigning it to the work of the Evil One. But their eyes have been blinded and their ears blocked by the very one whom they fear, and I want to say to them, '*ephphatha!*' Ignatius tells us that it's easy to be misled by the 'angel of darkness' in our desire for God (Mark. 4.12). Satan will often take on the guise of something good then try, little by little, to disturb the soul seeking what is good, for he is the father of lies and will often come, as Ignatius says in his 'Guidelines for the Discernment of Spirits', pretending to be an angel of light.

Place your mind in your heart

So while it's important to be present to Jesus in daily life, it's equally important to realize this must involve setting aside time for the *inner* journey ('Then were their eyes opened' Luke 24.31). We so often live on the surface, and our identity can consist of the parts we play in different circumstances rather than finding ourselves in him, as St Catherine of Genoa (not to be confused with her namesake of Sienna) reminded us, in the place of being still before God, with an open and longing heart. Yet the lure of activism is difficult to avoid, and priestly life increasingly seems to avoid attention to the heart. To be true to their calling, priests need to stand against this temptation and work for that inner conversion, be it their own, the hearts of those committed to their cure or those among whom they work and live. Are we forgetting this? We need to remember that our mind needs to be enfolded in the quietness of the heart, not in order to dismiss our reasoning faculties but that they should not dominate. For it is from the heart, rather than from the head, that true prayer emerges:

> *A pure heart create for me, O God,*
> *put a steadfast spirit within me.*
> *Do not cast me away from your presence,*
> *nor deprive me of your holy spirit.*
> *(Psalm 51.11f.)*

PRAYER AND MINISTRY

I often find that when priests begin to talk about their prayer, they talk about it in the context of the way it helps their ministry. Even contemplative prayer can be spoken of as a means of helping them feel less stressed. Of course, both those things are important (and it's good when priests begin to look at their prayer practice), but is the primary purpose of prayer to aid our ministry? Or is it to give expression to our desire for God? Remember the ordering of the two great Commandments ... While intercessory prayer might be connected with ministry, contemplative prayer is, primarily, concerned with opening us to the work of God deep within the heart. So let's consider the place of contemplative prayer in the life of the priest.

It can seem that contemplation is only appropriate for introverts, and those with a different personality type can feel unsuited to such prayer. There are many forms of prayer that appeal to the senses (e.g. singing psalms, listening to music, using the body in prayer, etc.), but there's a danger that extraverts will become dependent on external forms or experience burn-out because of the amount of activity in which they engage. We need to be careful of becoming dependent on stimulating felt experiences to enable prayer; it's one thing to use them to still the heart and mind so that one is open to God and quite another when the desire is for the emotional experiences we might associate *with* prayer. We must move from wanting milk to desiring the solid food that comes as our relationship with God matures. Likewise, although there is a place for intercessory prayer, if our prayer remains associated with asking or thanking God for things, we'll never discover the costly riches that God has in store for us (Matt. 13.44f.), which can be accessed by that simple prayer of loving regard, of desiring that we might be at one in the Heart of God.

> *For God alone my soul waits in silence;*
> *from him comes my salvation.*
> *He alone is my rock and my salvation,*
> *my fortress; I shall never be shaken.*
> *(Psalm 62.1f.)*

Is a 'good' time of prayer to be measured by our feelings, even feelings of being close to God? Or is it to be understood as the way we have sought and struggled to give God our loving attention? Sadly, in some places, it seems that, as the Church gives more attention to 'successful outreach', the temptation to ignore the inner life becomes greater and the potential for ignoring the 'better part' (Luke 10.42) can be overlooked. 'Success' and 'growth' can become the yardstick by which a church is judged – and judges itself and its ministers. But there is enormous danger in ignoring the inner life of prayer, especially meditation or contemplation, which, I believe, are of immense importance in our present culture and which are gifts the Church can offer the world.

Prayer and overactivity

Many spiritual directors have observed that what often emerges in direction is not a desire to nurture these gifts but overwork. It's clear that burn-out and extreme fatigue afflict some clergy, and I've noticed that they can forget the importance of developing a healthy inner – spiritual – life. While therapy is essential for some, many would benefit from giving more attention to meditation. I've sometimes pointed out to those attracted by more extraverted prayer that they may be adding fuel to the fire of a life that is already over-energized. When prayer is dependent on feelings, there will always come a time when God withdraws any felt experience so that we can mature into wanting God for God's-self alone and not for what we might obtain. We come to that time when we must be drawn by faith, a time that can be hard, dark, dry and difficult, especially if we've been used to prayer producing rewards. Most parents come to the point when they stop giving their children what they scream and shout for, realizing the importance – the necessity – of helping them to quieten down, but I'm not sure this is realized by some clergy! Contemplative prayer is not, primarily, about 'healthy living', but a large body of research in neuroscience, medicine and the social sciences shows that even ten minutes of contemplative prayer each day can help relieve stress and prevent burn-out.[8] With all the resources we have, shouldn't the Church be at the forefront of those promoting and teaching this gift of God? If the secular world recognizes this, might it be a healthy idea for every church to offer times for meditation?

But if a minister is not aware of the importance of such prayer – and practising it, or learning to practise it – then it's possible that those in their care will remain ignorant. Many laypeople who come for direction lament the lack of any contemplative element in their churches. Some have even confided that requests to their vicar for some expression of this approach to prayer have been turned down.

Be silent, still, aware

The noise, speed and busyness of modern life can become addictive. These 'addictions' have long been recognized as enemies of the spiritual life, and the evil one is never more pleased than when he can keep us distracted in these ways; while God *can* be encountered in them, they can easily provide superficial diversions. It's noticeable that Jesus countered these by seeking out places of silence and solitude for prayer, and he taught his disciples the importance of developing an inner 'cell' for the 'prayer of the heart' (Matt. 6.6).

However, silence, stability and solitude are not the ends we are to seek; rather they're the means whereby we can give attention to the door to our 'inner cave'. Ultimately God is to be found in the 'sound of sheer silence' (1 Kings 19.12), and we must sit at the door to the cave of the heart if we are to know God and be present to him who transfigures all things in the cloud of unknowing (Luke 9.34–36).

The fact that much worship involves little silence is cited by some as the reason for giving up on the Church. Yet, increasingly, its importance *is* being realized through Julian Meetings, Contemplative Prayer apps, Centring Prayer groups, etc. But not, often, in public worship, and if it is ('We'll have a moment of silence'), that's just what it is! If priests are afraid of silence, no wonder it's not part of our worship – the children won't cope! In my parish we developed a contemplative Saturday evening Eucharist, which attracted parents and children, maybe because it offered an alternative to constant activity? After all, Genesis suggests that creation emerged from eternal silence, which ought to precede activity:

> *Be silent,*
> *still,*
> *aware,*
> *for there,*
> *within your heart,*
> *the Spirit is at prayer.*
> *Listen and learn,*
> *open and find*
> *heart,*
> *wisdom,*
> *Christ.*[9]

Prayer is not easy

When people say they fear contemplative prayer will give room to the devil, I begin to wonder if there might be an element, for some, of silence meaning they must face the apparent emptiness of their inner life or that they are fearful of what they might encounter. It can be hard to begin that journey, but of all people clergy must be prepared to let go of whatever causes them to avoid entering this inner 'treasure cave' where God's Spirit moves in darkness. In my experience as a Franciscan, while it was true that I had to face myself in contemplative silence, it was also where I discovered a most profound sense of belonging.

It's long been known that prayer is not an easy work, so the first thing is to create space in our lives so God can work within the heart/soul (Eph. 3.16f.). As the SSF Principles say:

> *Praise and prayer constitute the atmosphere in which sisters and brothers must strive to live. They must endeavour to maintain a constant recollection of the presence of God and of the unseen world. An ever-deepening devotion to Christ is the hidden source of their strength and joy. He is for them the one all-lovely and adorable, God incarnate, crucified and risen, whose love is the inspiration of service and the reward of sacrifice.*[10]

Yet the demands of ministry can marginalize prayer. So,

> *They must, therefore, always be on their guard against the constant temptation to let other work encroach upon the hours of prayer, remembering that if they seek in this way to increase the bulk of their activity it can only be at the cost of its true quality and value.*[11]

How hard that is for many of us!

Distractions in prayer

Distractions in prayer can also cause difficulties. When we enter into contemplative prayer, we realize what lies beneath – images, feelings, sensations, memories, all this and more – becomes present to us as we seek to be attentive to God. They can reach out to us – some we notice, some we don't – like unwanted white noise until it begins to fade away. Or these distractions can emerge and take our attention like images out of the fog. There will be times when we *do* need make a note of what surfaces, and it can be helpful to keep a pen and note-pad at your side. Is there something our subconscious wants us to know, a rich but normally hidden gem that we need to place carefully where we can attend to it later? Does it speak of faith, hope and love, or are these distractions, playing with us like so many children, teasing and tugging at our sleeves to join them? Or are they darker – the opposite of those gifts of God – doubt, fear, anger and all their companions, tempting us to give them our attention for in the silence they can descend more deeply into our heart? All this is quite normal, and meditation allows us to be aware of what lies beneath. At times, we will need to sift the wheat and the chaff; at others, we just watch it all go by as if we're looking out of a train window. In all this, what matters is that we desire to be given to the work of the Spirit who searches everything, and when we find ourselves being led by other spirits we should gently turn the eye of the soul back to God.

&

FELT ABSENCE OF GOD IN PRAYER

As the earlier freshness of prayer begins to wear off, it can lose its appeal and, apart from when joining with others, begin to be neglected. This has been described as a time of 'felt absence', where the sense of God's presence and activity disappears. We might begin to realize that our relationship with God has been somewhat dependent on results, something that can happen if our faith-development has involved a strong emphasis on prayer being an exhilarating activity where amazing things are expected to occur. That *can* be the way people are taught – it's an attractive approach, but it is ephemeral at best and can have real dangers. It's tragic to come across fervent young people who have become disillusioned with prayer because it's not as exciting as it once was. I always recall the woman I encountered on a Mission who had been taught by her pastor to pray for healing from depression: 'If you have enough faith you'll be healed,' he'd told her. Sadly, her prayer didn't seem to have been answered, her depression consequently became worse and she had spent many more years in therapy. And if ever a minister has prayed over you for release from homosexuality (no matter how well meant), you'll know how deeply disturbing and damaging that can be, especially if you're young and impressionable.

Of course, God *does* work within us, but in far subtler ways. Many find that prayer is more about entering into a place where one discovers a deep and, probably, wordless desire for God where we sense God's desire for us. Like Abram who responded to God's call to leave the known for the unknown, we need to let go of initially helpful forms of prayer and enter into a dark wilderness (Ps. 13). And in that wilderness God will not only begin to encounter us in ways we never expected, but he will also enable us to realize our own true identity.

Prayer is about entering ever more deeply into Christ's desire to encounter us and to be wholly absorbed by his love, and then to respond with ever greater freedom and generosity to his will. And if clergy haven't made this move, then those they serve are likely to remain in an understanding of prayer that will never answer their deepest needs.

> *For God alone my soul in silence waits.*
> *(Psalm 62.3)*

Poustinia

We may not have a room that can be set aside for prayer (though some build a garden 'poustinia');[12] nonetheless, we can all develop a physical 'prayer corner' in an appropriate room, which, with careful attention to the way it is designed, can be a focus for our prayer if we have no access to a church. We can also develop a 'cell of the heart' and go there as often as we wish to nurture our relationship with God (Matt. 6.6f.). On the bus or plane, at those odd moments when we suddenly find we have nothing to think about and the temptation to look at emails is strong, we can withdraw into our inner poustinia. It is a place we can furnish with virtues and seek to nurture graces – compassion and mercy, patience and kindness, etc. We can go there to sup with Jesus and feed on him. It's the place where we learn to trust him who loves us with an everlasting love and longs for us to love God in return. This place can become a fertile field in which the Word can take root and grow, where, like Mary, we can say 'Behold the handmaid of the Lord …'

Of all those drawn into the love of God it is the Beloved in the Song of Songs who testifies best to a passion for God and, whatever the origins, has given voice to the contemplative desire:

> *Upon my bed at night I sought him*
> *whom my soul loves.*
> *(Song of Songs 3.1)*

While we must pray to see and love him in those among whom we live and minister, we're first called to a deep and personal passion for Christ, a passion which must inform our prayer:

> *Although you have not seen him, you love him; and even*
> *though you do not see him now, you believe in him and*
> *rejoice with an indescribable and glorious joy, for you are*
> *receiving the outcome of your faith, the salvation of your*
> *souls. (1 Peter 1.8f.)*

O God, you are my God, for you I long;
for you my soul is thirsting.
My body pines for you
like a dry, weary land without water.
So I gaze on you in the sanctuary
to see your strength and your glory.
(Psalm 63.1–2)

When prayer becomes dull

Space for such silence often needs to be carved out of our busyness. A few years ago, I attended a conference for priests during which we were encouraged to develop 'Fresh Expressions' of spirituality in our parishes. As we discussed how this might be done, what caught my attention was the suggestion that we might develop these not just for others but also for our own benefit. As a consequence, I began to offer Holy Hour (prayer before the Blessed Sacrament), a monthly Rosary group and a weekly contemplative Vigil Eucharist on Saturday evenings. While none came to the Holy Hour, quite a number found the Rosary group and contemplative Mass helpful, but *I* certainly benefitted as my own spiritual life was enhanced. It meant I was factoring a weekly period of silence and stillness into my ministerial life.

&

THIRSTING FOR GOD

In the silent, whitewashed refectory of the Franciscan Monastery of St Mary at the Cross, deep in the Worcestershire countryside, there hangs a large crucifix beneath which, in red lettering, is written SITIO – *I thirst* – the words Jesus spoke at his crucifixion. For me, they express a profound understanding of Christian spirituality – a thirst for God and his reign. That 'thirsting' resonates throughout the psalms (42.2; 63.1; 143.6) and the priest, above all, must have that longing for God who alone can quench our deepest desires. The problem, for many of us, is that we can easily be distracted and turn to other forms of gratification to slake that thirst. We can be especially distracted by those enemies of the spiritual life, restlessness and its cousin noise. Yet God is the friend of silence (Wisd. 18.14–15a) and when we experience that thirst the only thing we can do is to wait in silence until God refreshes us (Ps. 62.1). Ultimately, prayer is not a thing we do but a thing we can become when the heart is filled with waiting and longing for a clearer vision of God.

> *When he* [sic] *spiritually matures, when he recognizes his own powerlessness and the ineffable love of God, he becomes calm and everything proceeds on its own. Everything becomes prayer. And so he is not praying only when he is in church, but his entire life becomes a prayer.*[13]

While that is the invitation for a monk, it must also inform those who seek to lead others to God. So one of the questions every priest must ask is: 'Do I thirst for God?' and 'how do I give expression to that thirst?' If the answer is 'I don't', then you'd better arrange to see a spiritual director!

Time for the Heart of Jesus

In *The Life and Doctrine of St Catherine of Genoa* her confessor offers us these moving words he recorded: 'I shall never rest', Catherine said, 'until I am hidden and enclosed in that Divine Heart wherein all created forms are lost, and, so lost, remain thereafter all Divine; nothing else can satisfy true, pure, and simple love'.[14] This understanding of prayer as an act of pure love is common among the mystics. Apart from Julian of Norwich writing of the way Jesus 'wraps and enfolds us in love',[15] Teresa of Avila, the great Spanish mystic, is also reputed to have written that prayer 'is an act of pure love: words are not needed. Even if sickness distracts from thought, all that is needed is the will to love.' Although there is no one definition of what prayer is, it must be related to the heart and to love. Even that prayer which might come from an act of the will must, eventually, be embraced by the heart. At Jesus' conception it could not be only the womb of Mary that received him; her heart also needed to be large enough to give a home to God.

We may not have given any attention to the Heart of Jesus, but the understanding that our priesthood needs to be being rooted there is one on which we might meditate. As the tasks of ministry become increasingly multifaceted, we need to turn to his Heart if we are not to find them exhausting. And if your life is split between a multitude of parishes or you're a worker priest or facing the demands of family life, let your heart be inclined to his breast rather than fixed on whether you are living up to your calling. Ministry can be so exhausting that it's easy to give up nurturing our personal 'love affair with God'. Yet we can never love God too much, for in turning the eye of our heart to God and allowing love to flow out, that will spill over into every other aspect of life. If we seek to love God above all else, then that love will embrace both our neighbour and our self. We know that we are charged, among other things,

> to teach and to admonish, to feed and to provide for the
> Lord's family, to search for his children in the wilderness
> of this world's temptations and to guide them through its
> confusions, so that they may be saved through Christ for
> ever. (Preface, Rite of Ordination to the Priesthood)

But, sadly, the Ordinal hardly mentions how nurturing our relationship with God needs to be fundamental to priestly life. Yet when that ceases to be the case, our vocation suffers, for once we're not people of prayer, the Divine dimension of life begins to wither. 'The less you pray, the worse it goes.'[16] Neglect of our spiritual life *can* easily lead to a sense of shame or inadequacy. People look to us to be women and men of prayer, but a time sometimes comes when we know, in our heart of hearts, that we're neglecting this essential commitment. Of course, there'll always be occasions when we have to attend to a vital task and periods of refreshment and relaxation are necessary. But that doesn't mean we neglect God, quite the contrary. Whatever St Paul meant when he said we must 'pray without ceasing' – and many find the *Jesus Prayer* with its constant repetition of the phrase 'Lord Jesus Christ, Son of God, have mercy on me, a sinner' in time with one's breathing immensely helpful – it's possible to develop an awareness of the presence of God in all things and begin to incline the eye of our heart to that presence. To allow our gaze to take in the 'God-dimension' of life at all times and in all places while recognizing the need to have one particular place where prayer is the focus.

Seeking and finding God in all things

Priests, called to be the 'aroma of Christ' (2 Cor. 2.15), have to live in many worlds: the Church, wider society and particular relationships. Some have to juggle a demanding secular career with parish ministry and others have onerous family responsibilities. So each of us needs to ask ourselves where we find our primary place for our encounter with God? For many of us, it will be the Eucharist that aids us in realizing God in all things and thus helps develop a way of looking at the world with the eye of the heart. St John Cassian, the fourth-century ascetic, said that while we must work for the reign of God on earth that work must emerge from a pure heart: 'For without purity of heart none can enter into that kingdom'.[17] If the priest is set on developing that purity of heart, which involves both contemplation *and* seeking to live out of the Beatitudes, it will influence all they do and keep them rooted in the Heart of Jesus and not carried away by any disordered desires.

Everyday contemplation: the example of the Little Brothers and Sisters of Jesus

For many, the charism of the Little Brothers and Sisters of Jesus offers a useful example of this call to contemplative living in the world. Inspired by the hidden life of Bl. Charles de Foucauld, it's in the everyday, ordinary things of life and in desert places that God is to be encountered. As a teenager, de Foucauld lost his faith, but he regained it when he served in the French army in Morocco and encountered the native Muslim tribes. Subsequently, he lived almost his entire life as a solitary among those tribes until his murder in 1916. Like Francis, whose life inspired his, Charles had no cell except the 'cell of the heart'. As he wrote to his friend Henry de Castries, on 14 August 1901: 'As soon as I believed there was a God I understood that my only choice was to live for him alone. My religious vocation dates from the same hour as my faith.' The Little Brothers and Sisters find their religious poverty, like that of many priests, involves a lack of silent places in which to pray, so they must seek to incarnate Christ in little ways through their hidden life. They know that living in charity and kindness towards others is an essential means of encountering God, fulfilling as it does Christ's command that 'those who love God must love their brothers and sisters also' (1 John 4.21). However, they also balance this with periods of silence and solitude, for those who witness to Christ also need to contemplate him.

Love divine, all loves excelling

The Mother of Jesus, of course, contemplated her Son and was able to say to the stewards at the feast: 'Do whatever he commands you.' Mary Magdalene contemplated her friend, wondered at his resurrected body and was the first to bear witness to his resurrection. And it was the beloved disciple who perceived him on the lakeside. All these had a passion for Jesus.

Yet, sometimes, the command to love God with all our heart, soul, strength and mind can seem very exclusive: 'Whoever loves father or mother more than me is not worthy of me, and whoever loves son or daughter more than me is not worthy of me; and whoever does not take up his cross and follow after me is not worthy of me. Whoever finds his life will lose it, and whoever loses his life for my sake will find it' (Matt. 10.37). It's one of the 'hard sayings' of Jesus, yet, on further reflection, it is one of the most beautiful and inspiring. For it is a forceful reminder that our gaze needs to be directed to the Heart of him from whom every human heart, which can become so misshapen, is to take its form. It's easy for us to be misled by those we love – even the most wonderful of lovers has their faults – and we need to have our own heart, the centre of our being, constantly refocused and remade. But the Heart of Jesus has no flaws and longs to refashion us in God's image and likeness. It's a Heart that desires us to love him with all *our* heart. Like Mary Magdalene, we are to return to that 'garden' and be present to the place where we know him to be, hoping to be surprised by God. It is enough to be there.

Prayer is like watching for the
Kingfisher. All you can do is
Be where he is likely to appear, and
Wait.

Often, nothing much happens;
There is space, silence and
Expectancy.
No visible sign, only the
Knowledge that he's been there,
And may come again.
Seeing or not seeing cease to matter,
You have been prepared.
But sometimes, when you've almost
Stopped expecting it,
A flash of brightness
Gives encouragement.[18]

When such a moment comes, it's a moment of sheer grace when we've been given the privilege to see through all the distractions into the Heart of God. If that moment comes to you, then it's not something *outside* you but something inside, something you can return to and relish.

Questions for reflection

- Do I thirst for God? How do I give expression to that? What do I need to help me develop that thirst?
- Do I avoid giving time to prayer and, if so, why might that be?
- Do I need to seek out places of silence and solitude?

Notes

1 Attributed to St John of the Cross, in Gilbert Shaw, *A Pilgrim's Book of Prayers*, SLG Press, 1992 [1945], p. 78.

2 St John Damascene, *De fide Orthodoxa* 3.24; in *Patrologia Graeca* 94, 1089C.

3 St Augustine, *Confessions, Lib I.1.1*; in *Corpus Scriptorum Ecclesiasticorum Latinorum* 33, 1–5.

4 *The Cloud of Unknowing*, ch. 6.

5 A paper by Robert Jeffery, 'Imitating Christ: Wesley's Christian Pattern and Spirituality for Today', given at the Methodist Sacramental Fellowship Public Meeting during the Methodist Conference of 2006 in Edinburgh.

6 F. P. Harton, *Christian Dhyāna: or, Prayer of Loving Regard. A Study of 'The Cloud of Unknowing'*, SPCK, 1930.

7 Brother Lawrence (1605–91), *The Practice of the Presence of God*.

8 Matt and Kim Bloom, *Flourishing in Ministry research initiative*, Lewis Centre for Church Leadership, 2017.

9 An inscription said to have been found in a ruined English convent.

10 Principles of the Society of St Francis, Day 14, in *Daily Office SSF*, Mowbray, 1992, p. 305.

11 Principles SSF, Day 16.

12 Poustinia: the Russian word for 'desert' also used to designate a small cabin or room set aside for silence and prayer. See Catherine Doherty, *Poustinia*, Madonna House Publications, 1975.

13 Archimandrite Vasileios of the Iveron Monastery, Mount Athos, 2011, 'Everything is Prayer', *The Orthodox Word*, No. 279, pp. 158–170.

14 *The Life and Doctrine of St Catherine of Genoa*, ch. XIV.

15 *Revelations of Divine Love*, ch. 5.

16 John Chapman, *Spiritual Letters*, Burns & Oates, 2003, ch. 38 (used by permission of Bloomsbury Publishing Plc).

17 St John Cassian, *Conferences* 1, ch. 4.

18 Ann Lewin, 'Disclosure', in *Watching for the Kingfisher*, Canterbury Press, 2009.

6

Seven Times a Day I Praise You

The Daily Office

୬

*Every clerk in Holy Orders is under obligation, not being
let by sickness or some other urgent cause, to say daily the
Morning and Evening Prayer, either privately or openly.
(Canon C26, 55)*

୬

*Let my prayer rise before you as incense,
the lifting up of my hands as an evening sacrifice.*[1]

Well maybe not seven times, no matter what the psalmist
said (119.164). Although the origins of monastic life were
connected with a desire to live out St Paul's injunction to
'pray without ceasing', most religious (let alone clergy) these
days don't find it possible to pray the sevenfold Office (the
'official' prayer of the Church comprising mainly psalms and
other scriptural readings) of Matins, Lauds, etc. However, the
Daily (or Divine) Office offers a treasury full of rich resources
to aid our relationship with God, and it's no wonder that
clergy are obliged to pray it.

The place of the Office in the life of the Church

Rooted in earlier Jewish forms of daily prayer, the Office is
intended to consecrate different parts of the day, seasons and
life, sanctifying time and keeping us from a form of prayer that

might be dependent on our moods rather than the revelation of God. Some versions of the Office order the psalms in a way that reflects this, but all connect us with the whole Body of Christ, living and departed, and help us remember that Body holding us close to the saints: the great Teresa and the Little Flower, Josephine Butler and the Martyrs of Uganda – we welcome them and enter their prayer. It educates the subconscious and, when said corporately and with attention, profoundly unites us. As someone whose prayer was deeply affected by this rhythmic recitation, 'mindfully' slowly – oh, so slowly at times – and quietly, I know the effect it has and how it can draw others into it, as is witnessed by the many who are drawn to join with Religious as they pray the Office. Through this prayer, we share in the worship which the Church and the whole of creation offers to the glory of God (Ps. 66.4), a paean shared between Office and Eucharist, which, like the two sides of a choir, complement and inform each other, filling each out that both may be enriched. Many consider the identity of the Church of England and, by extension the Anglican Communion, to have been profoundly formed by the centrality of the Divine Office. Whatever 'fresh expressions' we might develop, I pray that the Church doesn't neglect this charism because it's our unique gift to the life of the People of God.

One of the challenges of priestly spirituality is how to develop a rhythm of life whereby God can animate every aspect of our identity, transforming us into a true *imago Dei*. This concerns not just the personal but also the institutional, for when the priest prays it is both as an individual *and* as an icon of Christ's body. And while that applies equally to the laity, it applies particularly to those set apart to pray for those in their care. There's a wonderful meditation by the eleventh-century St Norbert of Xanten (1080–1134), which Michael Ramsey shared in *The Christian Priest Today*:

O Priest, what are you?
You are not from yourself, for you are from nothing;
you are not to yourself,
because you are a mediator to God;
what therefore are you? Nothing and everything,
O Priest.

So priests have a duty and a responsibility to pray the prayer of the Church not just for themselves but in and for the whole church. As John Cosin, the post-Reformation Bishop of Durham, wrote:

> *We are to remember that we which are priests are called 'angeli domini'; and it is the angel's office not only to descend to the people and teach them God's will, but to ascend also to the presence of God, to make intercession for the people, and to carry up the daily prayers of the church in their behalf as they are bound to do.*[2]

One of the glories of the Office is its ability to take us out of the particular moment we find ourselves in and plunge us into the glorious sweep of Divine revelation. Unconcerned with how we may feel, it draws us into that redemptive dynamic, inviting us to let go of ourselves and allow the hopes and fears, sorrows and joys, pain and wonder, sadness and desire that we find recounted in Scripture to carry us. That dynamic is always, in the end, hopeful and faithful. Not that personal prayer hasn't a place, far from it. Rather our commitment to the Office means that prayer is not merely dependent on us and our feelings. It is, in a sense, the 'skeleton' which holds the body together, the 'bones and sinew' of our spiritual life.

Ora et labora

While St Benedict spoke of *ora et labora* (prayer and work) as fundamental to the life of a monk, the Rite of Ordination also makes it clear that prayer is part of the work of a priest. Until it closed in 1995, ordinands at Lincoln Theological College passed beneath an arch bearing those words as they entered chapel. However, it can be easy for us to begin to think that the 'real' work of the day begins as we *leave* the oratory. Do we, perhaps, approach the Office as a task to be done, rushed through from a sense of duty or even neglected altogether? Or as a feast that can nourish us?

WHEN THE OFFICE LOSES ITS FRESHNESS

Much of this chapter was written during a stay at the Anglican Franciscan Monastery of St Mary at the Cross at Glass-hampton. For 25 years I had, as a brother, prayed the Office each day with others; at times just 2 or 3 of us, at others maybe 20. Now I do so on my own, but this place reminds me that one never does pray alone but always as part of that great company of witnesses who stand before the throne of God day and night (Rev. 7.15). That is my first reflection when someone says to me that the Office has lost its fresh-ness: remember that it joins you to that great company of voices that embrace you in prayer and let yourself really be present to them.

'I don't need to say the Office'

No, you don't. You need to *pray* it.

In 2014 a research project into the place of the Daily Office among Anglican clergy was carried out, which includes an observation worth quoting in full:

One cleric I spoke to ... commented that after mentioning to his bishop that he found the obligation of saying the daily Office tedious and unhelpful, the bishop had responded by releasing him from it and they agreed that a praying of a daily Examen would be a suitable replacement. While ... I have found the Examen of great personal use over the years, actually I believe the Office has not only a wider significance and usefulness within the body of the Church but also is the greater resource of the two, not least because an Office can and usefully does contain an Examen but an Examen does not contain an Office nor its constituent elements.[3]

While there are many different forms of prayer, the writer noted the imperative of the Daily Office while observing that:

there would seem to be a crisis, or at least a challenge, in the way the institution of the Church explains and presents the Office to those in training for ordination ... Notions of teaching and discipline around personal and daily prayer that were reclaimed by the Anglican Church in the nineteenth century ... appear to have been relinquished during the course of the latter part of the twentieth century ... Where the obligation of the Office is communicated it is largely a matter of instruction about the required routine with no clarification of the creative flexibility and possibilities of its form and content and no sense of inspiration deriving from its potential and its ultimate part in God's invitation into mature Christian freedom and at-one-ment with his son, Jesus Christ.[4]

As someone who has prayed the Office for over 50 years, sometimes more out of duty than desire, I find myself agreeing with that piece of research, but I realize that there are ways that can help or hinder us in our praying.

Joining with an unseen host

First, the way we prepare for the Office, like anything else, is important. In community we were encouraged to arrive in good time and silently recall that we were about to share in a ceaseless round of prayer and praise. Now that I do not pray with others, I try to begin by recalling that I'm *not* alone but the Holy Ones welcome me just as the Brothers, here, welcome me as a guest in their choir. I also find that offering a brief prayer of intent can also be of help.

A PRAYER BEFORE THE OFFICE

Lord, I offer you this prayer and praise,
together with that of angels and saints.
May all the words of this prayer be acts of love,
adoration, thanksgiving and surrender
to your holy will.
And may it be a sacrifice of praise and glory to you,
O Blessed Trinity. Amen.

That 'waiting on God' extends beyond the Office. If a time of silence after formal prayer is observed (as it is here), it can take us into another realm. Yesterday evening, guests and Brothers gathered in the narthex after Evening Prayer to remain before the Blessed Sacrament exposed to our gaze on the altar. We were there waiting, silently and patiently, on God. To the outer senses, nothing 'happened'. Yet this silent 'gazing on God', of course, opens us to the One who gazes on us. We might (will) get distracted: my inner eye may be fixed on the Host or on the written psalm, but where is my heart, my attention?

Preparation of place

The place where prayer is offered can be as varied as a monastery chapel, a railway carriage or a park bench. Clearly it helps if the place has something about it that assists us in focusing on the Divine, but where that's not possible we still need to prepare ourselves by taking a moment to recall what we're about to do and to focus our attention by deeply breathing in the Spirit of God and breathing out all that we're carrying that might distract us. As the SSF Principles say, 'it is of little value to be present at the common devotions in a formal or careless spirit. They [the brothers and sisters] must seek to make of each office an offering of true devotion from the heart' (Day 16). It's also helpful to form an intention in saying the Office. For whose benefit might I, with loving devotion, offer this prayer? Then, maybe, light a candle, use a prayer stool, settle in front of an icon, burn some incense. Be silent ... still ... aware ...

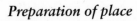

THE BODY AT PRAYER

Sitting, standing, bowing, kneeling

All remind us of the importance of the body in prayer. Corporate action in worship can be deeply moving, but have you noticed how we seem to be an increasingly sedentary church stuck to the pews and only rising to sing a hymn or chorus? We seem to have forgotten that our body needs to carry and express our prayer as well, something that our Orthodox sisters and brothers can teach us. From traditional acts such as bowing at the Holy Name to the sign of the cross over lips and heart and deep bows at the Gloria or letting our bodies 'pray the prayer', especially the Our Father, what we do can help prayer. The ancient tradition of standing enables the body to pay attention and shows both respect and equality with another. I've noticed that when congregations, having been invited to enter into the drama of the Eucharistic Prayer or the Our Father, promptly sit down I experience a real sense of disconnection, especially if I'm presiding, and I begin to feel as if I'm facing an audience! By contrast, when I and the people stand together, there's a real sense that we're all part of that Divine drama.

હ

PRAYING THE OFFICE

The psalms

The psalms speak out of the reflective, sometimes emotive, heart of the psalmist(s). They are at times encouraging, challenging, comforting, affirming. Here one finds hate and love, passion and praise, adoration and sorrow, penitence and longing and so much more. How wonderful their un-ashamed inclusion of all human emotions! How delightful to be caught by the odd phrase or line – to find oneself, for example, relishing the thought that 'My boundaries enclose a pleasant land' (Ps. 16.6). How rich their inclusion of God's presence in all things – storm and wind, trees and rocks, rivers and oceans. And when one does pray without another human presence, it's always possible to stop when those moments occur and savour them. In the fourth century, St Athanasius the Great described the psalms as a 'garden' containing all kinds of fruits.[5] When I step outside the monastery and my eye takes in the beauty of the Worcestershire countryside, I am swept up in the psalmist's cry:

The heavens declare the glory of God,
and the firmament proclaims the work of his hands.

Day unto day conveys the message,
and night unto night imparts the knowledge.
(Psalm 19.1)

John Calvin said that the psalms act like a 'mirror' to the soul.[6] No wonder, then, that they occupy so much of the Office and why we need to cherish and *relish* them. I want to suggest there are at least three levels at which they can be prayed that might be helpful.

Praying the psalms

First, there's the level of pure recitation where the words simply 'carry' us, where the subject of the psalm is the one who prays it: 'In God alone is my soul at rest; my help comes from him' (62.1). We are using the words of the psalm to express something to God but not necessarily what we feel; our feelings are taken into the dynamic of the psalmist's prayer.

Second, we can enter *into* the words – let ourselves inhabit them. Allow yourself to be caught up in pleasure and pain, joy and grief, etc. and use them as a means of intercession. Let them be a go-between, an *inter-cede*; expanding your heart that it might grow and encompass more than you can conceive. Know that the hate and fear which the psalmist expresses are also known by God who is aware of all things and grow in confidence in knowing his presence in all things. This is also the way of praying the psalms which allows us to enter into Jesus' prayer to his Father. We can legitimately place ourselves into the heart of Christ as he prays and, in this way, be detached from self and given to the Other.

Third, we can pray 'beneath' the words. We can notice how they move us as we pray them and allow that deeper movement: 'Preserve me, God, I take refuge in you. I say to the Lord: "You are my Lord. My happiness lies in you alone"' (16.1). We can notice the joy there might be in our heart, even though we may not have been aware of it. And, if alone, we may spend a moment or two relishing those feelings.

The psalms provide a rich source of imagery, a treasury of desire, appeal, challenge and confidence. They allow us – and remind us that it's OK – to express negative as well as positive feelings to God. There's an integrity about them which means we're never left in a hopeless place. The trouble, often, lies in the *way* they're said or sung. Rather than being a meditation, I sometimes feel they're approached as a script to be got through as quickly as possible! In community, we were taught four important norms as to how they should be recited:

- Say them unhurriedly.
- Use the colon to allow a reflective pause. How long? About three seconds.
- If said with others, remember this is a communal act, not a private devotion. Listen to the person nearest to you and speak in time with each other. And …
- Don't dominate. If you can't hear the person next to you, you're not listening, you're speaking too loudly. And that, of course, is a useful reminder to clergy about how we are to live … *sotto voce*.

While we often say them they were, of course, written to be sung, and the early Christian communities maintained that tradition (Eph. 5.19). So if you can, try singing them to a simple chant. Singing has been recognized as an aid to prayer and while it would appear Augustine didn't actually compose the aphorism often attributed to him, *whoever sings prays twice*, nonetheless many find using the modern psalm tones or plainsong melodies helpful in enabling the Spirit to pray in them. And remember, the psalms are not intended to be sung to the glory of the musicians but that glory might be given *to the Father, and to the Son, and to the Holy Spirit ...*

In these and other ways, it is Christ to whom we need to direct our attention as we pray the psalms. He is the one who is there, in the background if you like: the ground from which the psalms are to flourish. Yet each member of the Trinity has their place as we conclude with the wonder of the doxology:

Glory to God, Source of all being,
Eternal Word and Holy Spirit.

As we acclaim that, we remind ourselves that our recitation takes us out of the here and now and places us in the flow of eternal time:

As it was in the beginning, is now,
and ever shall be, world without end. Amen.

Praying with Scripture

The way we approach praying the psalms can also apply to the rest of Scripture. In the Prologue to his Rule, Benedict said that we need to 'incline the ear of our heart' in order to turn our 'saying' the Office into praying the Office. I found one simple way in which this can be done when I was in SSF: we left a minute's space after a reading. which was never declared 'ended'. The word was simply allowed to enter into silence ... In that silence, I would simply sit with the Word and notice how it challenged or moved me, what it said to me, asked of me or invited me to consider. And, for me, behind those reflections to desire that the Word forms me more into the likeness of Christ. So, when I am giving my attention to this Divine reading, I need to ask that my heart be more open to receiving the Word and, when the Word has 'spoken', to engage in conversation. Or I simply hold the

Word in my heart so that, in the silence, it can permeate me more and more. Of course, all that is based on the Benedictine practice of *lectio divina* and, while the Office may not always be the right place for it to be practised, the principle – slowly reading aloud and then allowing silence, noticing what takes your attention, speaking to God about that in your heart and then resting in silence – offers a means of being nourished by the word. A simple form of *lectio* is provided in Appendix 5.

Of course, this prayerful, reflective reading of the Scriptures can be difficult when there's a huge 'chunk' of it to devour, so I wonder if you might abbreviate the passage or chose an alternative Lectionary?

In Christ alone

For many years now, I've prayed the Office alone. Yet when I enter into that sacred space I know that I am not alone: Christ is with me, the saints are present and I will be praying with others around the world. I am bonded with them all, for the veil between heaven and earth is opened as we pray (Heb. 12.22–23). And if, at the start of the day, I find myself wanting to roll over and go back to sleep, or when there's just so much else to do and I'm tempted to skip prayer, I remember these words attributed to Fr Pedro Arrupe SJ, sometime Superior General of the Jesuits who died in 1991:

> *Nothing is more practical than finding God, than falling in Love in a quite absolute, final way. What you are in love with, what seizes your imagination, will affect everything. It will decide what will get you out of bed in the morning, what you do with your evenings, how you spend your weekends, what you read, whom you know, what breaks your heart, and what amazes you with joy and gratitude. Fall in Love, stay in love, and it will decide everything.*[7]

SEVEN TIMES A DAY I PRAISE YOU

Questions for reflection

- How do I 'pray' the Office?
- St Benedict described the Office as the 'Opus Dei'. If it has become a chore, what might I need to do to help enliven it again?
- Do I need to talk about the way I pray the Office with my spiritual director?

Notes

1 *The Daily Office SSF*, 1992, The European Province of the Society of St Francis.

2 John Cosin quoted in P. More and F. Cross (eds), *Anglicanism*, SPCK, 1935, pp. 628–9.

3 Andrew S. Walker, 'The Usage, Understanding and Theology of the Daily Office Amongst Anglican Clergy Today', PhD thesis in Theology and Mission, King's College, London, 2014, pp. 134f.

4 Walker, 'The Usage, Understanding and Theology of the Daily Office', pp. 162f.

5 *The Letter of Athanasius to Marcellinus on the Interpretation of the Psalms*.

6 *Commentary on the Psalms*, 1557.

7 *Finding God in All Things: A Marquette Prayer Book*, Marquette University Press, 2009.

7

Eucharistic Living

The sacrament of cosmic communion

*Will you endeavour to fashion your own life ...
according to the way of Christ, that you may be a
pattern and example to Christ's people?
(Ordination of Priests: The Declarations)*

*The cup of salvation I will raise;
I will call on the Lord's name
(Psalm 115.13)*

Holy living

Most people, if they ever give it a thought, probably consider the Eucharist a service you go to on a Sunday morning.
Sometimes. A few find they're drawn to be present at a quiet
mid-week celebration. But for others it's the centre around
which their lives revolve; whenever the Church recalls, in
word and action, how Christ commanded us to *do this in
memory of me* they are drawn to be present. Most of us
realize how great and humbling is the privilege of presiding at
the Eucharist for the essence of the priesthood is *astare coram
te et tibi ministrare* (to stand and minister in the name of
the Lord),[1] a calling realized at the altar and the workplace.[2]
So what place might this Sacrament play in our spirituality?

How might it be something we don't simply *preside* at but which we *live* through – live out of?

Presiding and praying

There have been times when clergy complain that having to 'lead the service' means they can't pray as they once did and that they've lost touch with God in worship; there's so much preparation to be done and so much to think about that they can't pray. When I hear this said, I'm inclined to ask them what it might be like for the congregation! If we've come to think of ourselves as those who lead rather than enable worship and if we're more concerned to hold people's attention by keeping them engaged with ever more sophisticated staging, lighting, etc. might something have gone wrong? Some worship leaders are beginning to feel they are presiding over 'Sunday productions'³ that have little relevance to those seeking to encounter God. At such times, I gently begin to explore what would help *them* to worship prayerfully – because if the 'worship leader' can worship prayerfully, they might help others in their similar desire.

However, if the context concerns presiding at the Eucharist, I might say to them – *and nor should you!* For you have been given the enormous privilege, the great honour, of praying the words of our Lord and Master. You speak those words which are spoken eternally; you open the curtain onto the mysteries of heaven and stand where angels and archangels stand, bowing with them before our Maker. What greater gift could God give you? What more wonderful place could you inhabit? As Bishop Michael Ramsey wrote:

> *In taking, breaking and consecrating (the priest) acts in Christ's name and in the name not only of the particular congregation but of the Holy Catholic Church down the ages ... he finds that at the altar he is drawn terribly*

and wonderfully near not only to the benefits of Christ's redemption but to the redemptive act itself.[4]

Priest and people are one whenever the mysteries are celebrated. Whoever presides is as much part of the body that is offered and offers itself as any other part. It is Christ who is the Host, the one who feeds us; and Christ is the One on whom we feed.

THE ICONIC NATURE OF THE PRIESTHOOD

The priest as an alter Christus

The priest, then, when presiding at the Eucharist is one with Christ our great High Priest. But how often do we allow ourselves time to meditate on that calling as we stand at the altar and give utterance to the Word? As we stand there, we are not simply Tom or Mary, we are an *alter Christus* – another Christ – profoundly united to the Word of the Father. Though we may only be a 'little Christ', nonetheless we are to be configured to him *by* whom and *with* whom and *in* whom we are to become Christlike. What might his life, passion, death and resurrection say about our lives? This speaks into the heart of priestly spirituality, not in the way the term has been used to argue that only a man can be ordained to the priesthood, but because we are *all* called to 'put on Christ' (Rom. 13.14). Christ, through baptism, dwells in my head, hands, feet – and especially my heart. And I dwell in him. Our priestly calling means we, especially, must let go of our 'false self' that the 'true (Christ) self' might inhabit us (Gal. 3.28). The Roman Catholic rite of Ordination makes this clear in a telling instruction to candidates: 'imitate the mystery you celebrate: model your life on the mystery of the Lord's cross.'[5]

On taking the chasuble
Lord, you have said, 'My yoke is sweet and my
burden light';
grant that I may so carry it as to merit your grace. Amen.

The priest as an icon of Christ

As priests 'put on' Christ (Rom. 13.14), they become an icon of him by virtue of their sacramental ordination. Whether we like it or not, many will see them as 'walking sacraments' and assume they'll see in them what they expect to see in every Christian. So when a priest, in particular, is found to be an abuser (in whatever sense), it's a great and terrible tragedy for not only do they harm their victims but, ultimately, it is Christ who is abused. While none of us is or can be perfect, nonetheless priests must be aware of how their patterns of behaviour can damage that Divine image.

What is an icon?

You probably know that the word derives from the Greek 'εἰκών' (*eikon*) meaning an image or representation. When associated with a sacred image, it is not meant to be a realistic or dimensional representation but to reveal what the inner eye of faith sees so that what it portrays becomes apparent. It's a 'window into heaven', the image of another reality created through particular sacred practices including prayer and fasting. Remembering that it is not themselves they are to proclaim but Jesus Christ, priests are to help conform others into the image of the One they serve, a process that takes time – years – but this conforming to the image of Christ lies at the heart of priestly vocation. That is why the chasuble is worn: just as newly baptized Christians are traditionally clothed in a white garment, so the chasuble covers the person who inhabits it with the symbolic cloak of Christ's priesthood thus reminding all Christians that we are to 'put on the Lord Jesus Christ' (Rom. 13.14).

Mary, mother and priest?

Now what follows might be a bit controversial for some, but did you know that there are icons and mosaics, dating back to at least the sixth century, which show Mary clothed in the priestly chasuble and that there is an ancient tradition that the Annunciation acted as her ordination? Or that, over the centuries, people have noted that the motherhood of Mary is a type of the priesthood? For she who bore, gave birth to, nourished, listened to, suffered with (her soul was pierced), stood by Jesus as he died and knew deep sorrow as well as joy reveals a type of the priest. In gazing at the fruit of her womb and saying 'this is my body ... my blood', a woman utters what can only be known to those of her gender and, for centuries, a rich spirituality connected with the priesthood of Mary flourished.[6] She who declared herself to be the handmaid of the Lord presents a potent spirituality to priests, whatever their gender, for she offers an image that speaks into the heart of the priesthood. Some will find that a powerful insight, while others, who may not have considered Mary in connection with priestly spirituality, might reflect on what she may have to offer them.

> Kind Queen of Heaven, lend thy little hand,
> And I will press upon it such a kiss
> Of homage, reverence, and loyalness
> As only heaven's courtiers understand.

I kiss thy priestly hand, so strong, so fair,
Handling so oft the Body of Christ.
He hides Himself from me in Eucharist,
He lay upon thy lap and stroked thy hair.
(Fr Andrew SDC, 'The Queen's Hand')

Perhaps we might take as our own the petition authorized by
Pius X in 1906: 'Mary, Virgin priest, pray for us.'

The Church as the icon of Christ

Ultimately, we're all invited to be icons of Christ. Priests, who
are assumed to have a familiarity with Divine things, need to
be growing into the likeness of him whom others look to us
to reveal. We need to nurture our spiritual life by keeping
ever fresh our desire for God, which becomes sacramentally
evident in the Eucharist as we become one with that which
we celebrate.

❧

CELEBRATING THE MYSTERY

Anglicanism embraces a wide theological spectrum and, consequently, a variety of spiritualities, so some of you might find
all this is rather different from what you are familiar with.
You might also not know of some of the priestly traditions
associated with the Eucharist, which can be invaluable in
helping the priest pray. So what follows is offered in the hope
that it might be of help to all who have the immense privilege
of presiding at these mysteries.

Preparing

Preparing, both on the day itself but also beforehand, is
clearly important and this can be aided by the Examen. There

are many preparatory prayers that can be of help which are available online or which appear in devotional books and the practice of forming an 'intention' can help focus our prayer: is there a person or cause you wish to remember or a grace *you* need to ask for?

The tradition of fasting for an hour beforehand is a reminder that our bodies aid our prayerful preparation.

Vesting

Sacristies (or vestries) can become busy and noisy places, so how might we enable a quieter atmosphere in this 'antechamber' to the Mysteries? If the priest realizes the importance of being recollected, then those who assist in the celebration might be encouraged to develop a similar stillness of heart and mind – a stillness not of emptiness but of waiting, like Elijah (1 Kings 19.12f.), for God to become present. After all, the vesting performed by the priest is not just a matter of changing clothes but an action redolent with symbolic meaning and, ideally, should never be done in a hurried or thoughtless manner. From the vestments of the Temple priests (Ex. 28) to the virtues with which Christians are to be attired (Eph. 6.11ff.) what the priest wears speaks about who they are and who they are called to become (Col. 3.19ff.). Vestments are not merely uniforms, although they serve a similar purpose of showing to what we're called, nor are they merely robes chosen according to whim. So you'll find in Appendix 6 some prayers associated with each item, which can aid the sacred ministers in gradually 'clothing' themselves in Christ. It is for this reason that, in the Orthodox churches, the priest kisses each vestment. And while George Herbert probably had Ephesians 6.13f. in mind when he composed his great poem, 'Aaron', it is oddly suggestive of vesting, reminding us that it is Christ who hosts this Sacred Feast:

Holinesse on the head,
Light and perfections on the breast,
Harmonious bells below, raising the dead
To lead them unto life and rest:
Thus are true Aarons drest.

Profaneness in my head,
Defects and darknesse in my breast,
A noise of passions ringing me for dead
Unto a place where is no rest:
Poore priest thus am I drest.

Onely another head
I have, another heart and breast,
Another musick, making live not dead,
Without whom I could have no rest:
In him I am well drest.

Christ is my onely head,
My alone onely heart and breast,
My only musick, striking me ev'n dead;
That to the old man I may rest,
And be in him new drest.

So holy in my head,
Perfect and light in my deare breast,
My doctrine tun'd by Christ (who is not dead,
But lives in me while I do rest)
Come people; Aaron's drest.

Liturgy of the Word

As we come to the altar, which symbolizes Christ, there's a tradition that the priest kisses this sacred table, which, apart from anything else, expresses the desire of the congregation for union with him. Although it's important to welcome the people, remember they're to be welcomed on behalf of the Host (which is why the priest normally does this): it is not your celebration but his. Many of us invite a time of silence after the Greeting to recall that we all stand in the presence of the Divine Mystery and, in another period of silence, I like to invite the congregation to recall their sins as I, too, recall mine – I don't like to rush into the Confession.

Then there's the question of attention. Have you noticed that some congregations can give their entire attention to what appears in Liturgy booklets or a projector screen? It's like being in a play where the audience read the script rather than engage with the drama. How can we wean people off these and encourage them to attend to the action of the Liturgy? I sometimes wonder if we've forgotten the uniqueness of our faculty to *hear* as we give increasing attention to reading. If you haven't done so for a time, try putting down the Scripture reading, which is probably printed in a booklet. Instead, pay attention to what you hear and notice whether the word actually sinks into a much deeper place than can be accessed by reading. I recall an occasion many years ago when, prior to attending an Orthodox liturgy, I asked the priest for a Liturgy booklet to which he replied, 'Books, books, books! You Westerners always want books!!' Needless to say, I didn't get one. But I've always remembered his words and have tried to wean myself from – books. (The fact that he was a convert from Anglicanism needn't bother us too much ...)

More silence seems appropriate after the Word has been read; it's easy to forget the value of the faculty of hearing and listening to the reading can be an act of mindfulness. If you're presiding at a weekday Eucharist, perhaps the Homily might emerge from having listened to the Word in your heart.

Intercessor

Priests share in the ministry of 'he (who) always lives to make intercession for them' (Heb. 7.25). Called to stand before God with the people on our hearts, it is from the heart that prayer arises since contemplating another with the eye of the heart is to share in intercession for them. As Herbert reminds us in his poem, the priest is like Aaron who was called to enter into the Holy of Holies dressed in the sacred vestments, including the tunic bearing 12 jewels representing the 12 tribes of Israel (Ex. 28). It is in the Eucharist that we find the heart of priestly intercession most fully realized as the intentions we form and prayers we offer blend with Christ's offering. In realizing this, we are united with him who makes intercession for us in a profound way.

The Eucharistic Prayer

Here priest and people come to stand, in the presence of angels and archangels and the whole company of heaven, before the Throne of God, joining with them in the great song of the Thrice Holy (Rev. 4), where we realize ourselves as an instrument in the hands of God. In Christ we, as part of his Body, have entered beyond the curtain together with the whole assembly of the firstborn, and it is indeed no longer we but, through us, Christ who presides. We have moved from *chronos* to *kairos*, from time to eternity as we stand with all those robed in white (Rev. 7.9ff.). If you preside facing the people, let your gaze be on the mystical reality before you, Christ himself, and not just on the congregation. While we may need to keep one eye on the congregation, they must never so absorb our attention that we forget that our gaze needs to pierce through to Jesus.

As our celebration of the Divine Office shifts our gaze to the dynamic of the eternal, redemptive work of God, it's the Eucharist which focuses that dynamic in a sacramental way. It unites us with the whole company of heaven, with the Mother of Jesus and all those who are eternally present to the Presence. Such is the wonder of our calling that we need at this point to be deeply recollected and centred on him who is eternally present to us. I find the simple prayer said at the preparation of the chalice as wine and water are mingled together very helpful: 'By the mystery of this water and wine may we come to share in the divinity of Christ, who humbled himself to share in our humanity.' As the great Eucharistic Prayer unfolds, we need to consciously inhabit the words of Jesus and allow, at the end of the prayer, time for the 'prayer of silent regard' as we stand at the door that has been opened to heaven.

> *Raising our eyes to heaven, we pray:*
> *'My God, and my All!'*
> *(St Francis)*

There's a beautiful meditation on the Trinity by Richard Rohr OFM, which I'd like to share with you at this point:

> *The Mystery of (the) Trinity invites us into full partici-*
> *pation with God, a flow, a relationship, a waterwheel of*
> *always outpouring love. Trinity basically says that God is*
> *a verb much more than a noun. Some Christian mystics*
> *taught that all of creation is being taken back into this*
> *flow of eternal life, almost as if we are a 'Fourth Person'*
> *of the Eternal Flow of God or, as Jesus put it, 'so that*
> *where I am you also may be'.*[7]

As we stand in the presence of the Eucharistic Trinity, we become that 'fourth person' for our primary, baptismal call-ing is into this dynamic relationship with God whom we encounter as we celebrate with the whole company of heaven.

Saved by disability

I wonder if you've ever pondered the paradox that our redemption and salvation were not wrought through any *ability* that Jesus might have exercised – through his teaching, preaching, healing or miraculous activity – but through his *dis*ability, his being taken and broken for us? So at the supreme moment of union with him, we acknowledge that we can do nothing except follow his act of love, which is always the giving of one's self unto death – a white martyrdom (John 15.13). His sacrifice is eternally present, and through it we enter the Sanctuary of God where the Lamb is the Light and where the saints eternally sing 'You have redeemed us by your blood ...' (Rev. 5.19), yet we enter the Divine Presence through *his* brokenness, not our giftedness.

So whatever disabilities we may have, if allowed to inform our ministry, can communicate hope and trust to others who are also suffering. As one priest who suffers from a disability pointed out to me: 'this is a key gift of the priesthood in the midst of chaos and disaster. It's clearly not limited to those ordained priest, but it seems to me that priesthood models and exemplifies it. I think what people recognize and are held by is expressed in Julian's "All shall be well, and all shall be well, and all manner of thing shall be well"[8] – not the words obviously, but an underlying hope and trust.'

A *living sacrifice*

Our participation in this offering unites us with Christ's sacrifice. He has given me himself, united me with him – enfolded me in him – and I need to rest in that. There are times when I notice a deep and powerful longing to be consumed by Christ as I have consumed him as two lovers might desire to consume each other. To long to be part of him as he has become part of me. Is it from that deep and powerful place of longing that we're called to offer him our souls and bodies? Being a 'living sacrifice' can feel what priestly life is like, so I try to remember that, united with Jesus, I'm called to this 'holiness making' as we go out in the power of the Spirit to live and work to God's praise and glory – AMDG. As Christ gave himself for all, so must every priest. It's important, therefore, before ever we remove the outward garments of Christ to own, with deep thanksgiving, what we have celebrated.

❧

'MASS ON THE WORLD'

In the end, the Eucharist cannot be contained within the Church for it is greater than the liturgy we celebrate. Teilhard de Chardin SJ, the early twentieth-century palaeontologist, geologist, philosopher and priest, expressed this most profoundly in his great *Hymn of the Universe*, probably written on the Feast of the Transfiguration in 1923 when he was living in the Ordos Desert of Inner Mongolia. Lacking the necessities to say Mass, he was led to compose his majestic *Mass on the World*, which opens with one of the most remarkable statements ever made about the Eucharist as he realizes the need to raise himself beyond any symbols to offer all that lay before him 'up to the pure majesty of the real itself'.

He acknowledges that the words of Christ, spoken by the priest over bread and wine, flow beyond those forms to the whole Body of Christ. In fact, they reach into the cosmos itself so that all matter is affected by them. His Eucharist may lack bread and wine, but before him lie the elements of creation that will provide the substance for celebration. His prayer of consecration contains a wonderful invocation that the 'radiant word' would embrace and breathe life into the depths of creation so that Christ's hands might 'direct and transfigure' all that is brought into this Eucharistic act to remould, rectify: 'recast it down to the depths from which it springs'. Over what greater celebration could a priest preside?

Living Eucharistically

Teilhard reminds us that all are invited to 'live Eucharistically', to live out of that great sacrifice of prayer and praise and look at the world with wonder and awe, recognizing all things as a sacrament of the Divine. Is that what we hold on to as we leave the altar? He realized that Eucharistic spirituality overflows the Liturgy to embrace life itself and is made real as we seek to discern everyday holiness. The way we walk down the street with thankfulness in our hearts offering to God all that we encounter – the joys and sorrows, brokenness and wonder; the conversations we engage in, the sights that greet our eye whether that be in a green and pleasant place or among the houses, shops and factories of a neglected inner-city streetscape – all are the matter for our ongoing celebration. Our calling is to incline the heart to the real presence of Christ in all things.

Priestly spirituality, then, involves living with the intention of making of each moment an offering to God. The Eucharist is central to how our spirituality evolves because it is the nexus linking that which lies at the heart of our relationship with God and God's creation, the place where Divine Love is most fully revealed. To be lovers of God in all things must be the focus of our lives, not parishes, schools, cathedrals or whatever. They are the context. But we are called to love God and to live out of his compassionate Heart realizing that the life we celebrate is one that emerges from his sacrifice to which we are conjoined. Sacrifice is at the heart of priestly life, an 'Act of Communion'[9] with God in love. It is the means whereby we attain and rejoice in our true, Godly, life. At the altar, we join all our small sacrifices to his one saving sacrifice, and beyond the altar we seek to live sacrificially that we may share in the life of our great High Priest. For in Jesus we see how one person can belong utterly to God.

> *Father,*
> *I abandon myself into your hands;*
> *do with me what you will.*
> *Whatever you may do, I thank you:*
> *I am ready for all, I accept all.*
> *Let only your will be done in me,*
> *and in all your creatures –*
> *I wish no more than this, O Lord.*
> *Into your hands I commend my soul:*
> *I offer it to you with all the love of my heart,*
> *for I love you, Lord, and so need to give myself,*
> *to surrender myself into your hands without reserve,*
> *and with boundless confidence,*
> *for you are my Father.*
> *(Bl. Charles of Jesus, 'Prayer of Abandonment')*

Christ present in all people

Our particular calling is Eucharistic because we are to serve Christ present beneath the outward forms of those among whom we minister, wherever that may be. There is a way of loving people which begins to see in them the mystery in which they share, even though they may not realize this. I've always delighted in something Thomas Merton said as he recalled a moment walking down a street in Louisville:

> I was suddenly overwhelmed with the realization that I loved all these people; that they were mine and I theirs, that we could not be alien to one another even though we were total strangers. ... I have the immense joy of being man, a member of a race in which God Himself became incarnate. As if the sorrows and stupidities of the human

*condition could overwhelm me, now that I realize what
we all are. And if only everybody could realize this! But
it cannot be explained. There is no way of telling people
that they are all walking around shining like the sun.*[10]

> *The world is charged with the grandeur of God.
> It will flame out, like shining from shook foil. ...
> (G. M. Hopkins, 'God's Grandeur')*

But it's not easy in the humdrum routine of daily life. What
often happens as we walk down the street or sit on the train is
that we notice life, shrug our metaphorical shoulders or cross
our arms and get into a conversation with that 'evil spirit'
who happily waits just out of sight, ready to cast a critical
glare. He plays some old tapes about how awful things are
and gently leads us down the spiral into the place of darkness. It's then that we need to wake up and realize that the
sursum corda is not only necessary in the Liturgy: we are not
to look on the world with a critical glare but a contemplative
gaze. And when we catch ourselves going down that spiral,
we need to return to the simple spiritual practices which can
reawaken us to the wonder of creation – even though the
glory may be smeared with dirt:

> *May you be well;
> May you be happy;
> May you know the compassion of Christ.*[11]

Finally, I feel I can do no better than share with you another
reflection by Thomas Merton which challenges us to true
Eucharistic living:

> *If you are afraid to love, never become a priest, never
> say Mass. ... For when you begin to say Mass, the Spirit
> of God awakens like a giant inside you and bursts the*

locks of your private sanctuary. If you say Mass, you condemn your soul to the torrent of a love that is so vast and insatiable that you will never be able to bear it alone. That love is the love of the Heart of Jesus, burning within your own heart and bringing down upon you the huge weight of His compassion for all the sinners of the world.[12]

Questions for reflection

- What 'hymn' might I write that expresses my awareness of God's presence in all things?
- How can I develop that joy in seeing God in all things?
- In what ways might I deepen my awareness of the presence of God in the Eucharist?

Notes

1 Pope Benedict, Homily at the Chrism Mass, 2010.

2 'If you are Christians then your Jesus is one and the same: Jesus on the Throne of his glory, Jesus in the Blessed Sacrament, Jesus received into your hearts in Communion, Jesus with you mystically as you pray, and Jesus enthroned in the hearts and bodies of his brothers and sisters up and down this country. And it is folly, it is madness, to suppose that you can worship Jesus in the Sacraments and Jesus on the Throne of glory, when you are sweating him in the souls and bodies of his children. It cannot be done.' Frank Weston, Bishop of Zanzibar, from 'Our Present Duty', Concluding Address to the Anglo-Catholic Congress, 1923.

3 John Pavlovitz, 'Church, Here's Why People Are Leaving You. Part 1', Blogpost, 15 August 2014, available at https://johnpavlovitz.com/2014/08/15/church-heres-why-people-are-leaving-you-part-1/.

4 Michael Ramsey, *The Christian Priest Today*, SPCK, 2009, p. 10; emphasis mine.

5 Excerpt from the English translation of *The Ordination of Deacons, Priests, and Bishops*, ICEL, 1975. (© 1975, International Committee on English in the Liturgy, Inc. All rights reserved.)

6 Tina Beattie, 'Mary, the Virgin Priest?', *The Month*, no. 257, December 1996, pp. 485–493.

7 Richard Rohr, Daily Meditations, Center for Action and Contemplation, 12 May 2015, available at https://cac.org/trinity-2015-05-12/.

8 *Revelations of Divine Love*, ch. 27.

9 Fr Benson SSJE, quoted in the *Manual* of the Sodality of Mary, Mother of Priests, Day 8.

10 Thomas Merton, *Conjectures of a Guilty Bystander*, Image, 1966, pp. 156–157.

11 Spiritual Association of the Compassionate Hearts of Jesus and Mary.

12 Thomas Merton, 2014, *Selected Essays*, Orbis Books.

8

Living in Ordinary Time

Developing a wholesome life

You cannot bear the weight of this calling in your own strength, but only by the grace and power of God. (Ordination of Priests: The Declaration)

'It's so good to get back to ordinary time!' said one of my directees. What they meant was that after all the great Seasons the move into Ordinary Time can be a relief, allowing us to settle down and begin to work out our faith in the realities of daily living. Much has been written about various aspects of clergy well-being and I now want to consider a number of matters that might help us lead a 'healthy life'.

SPIRITUAL DIRECTION

I'm sure it's obvious that those charged with the care and formation of others need to take good care of their own, ongoing spiritual development. Those with the greatest pastoral responsibilities need the greatest pastoral – and spiritual – care, so if bishops, as well as clergy, make use of spiritual directors, confessors and supervisors, they're likely to let others know about the benefits of these ministries. But clergy *can* be tempted to go it alone, to say 'I don't need anyone telling me what to do' – a useful response if you want to avoid acknowledging aspects of yourself. But spiritual direction is a compassionate ministry which is rarely 'directive' and seldom concerns offering advice; rather, a director will gently help the directee (the person seeking help) notice what is preventing that freedom which is needed in order to respond in whatever way might be appropriate to the call of God; to engage in that process of discernment which sifts wheat and weeds; to wonder at the presence of God in all things, not least in my heart; to enable the directee explore their deepest desires.

What is spiritual direction?

Spiritual direction is a unique, privileged ministry the purpose of which is to enable the contemplative practice of helping the directee 'awaken to the mystery called God in all of life, and to respond to that discovery in a growing relationship of freedom and commitment'.[1] Some may combine spiritual direction with Confession and feel that the advice given is adequate for their spiritual needs, while others, whose director is a priest, may include Confession as part of direction. But it's important to realize the complementarity of the two ministries. They should not be confused for whereas the focus of the former is on liberation through the absolution of their sins and the grace that comes through this priestly ministry, the latter is concerned with the way God is moving in the life of the directee, a ministry open to all – lay or ordained – to exercise. It's the grace of a discerning spirit that enables this ministry, not the grace of ordination, and that spirit is available for all to receive.

There are also those who think that spiritual direction is only needed at times of crisis. But this isn't 'emergency treatment'; rather it's a necessary, ongoing relationship for healthy and holy living. Occasionally I've been asked to see priests at such moments, and it's never satisfactory – the accompanying assumptions, resistances and expectations can be great. It's in ongoing direction that a person can gain the confidence to 'be themselves' in the presence of another Christian knowing that the ministry is bounded by norms of confidentiality. While it doesn't enjoy the same 'seal' as the Confessional, what's said in that space stays in that place, unless the law requires otherwise.

It's also an important means of being accountable, before God, for who we are. Direction helps address the tendency to spiritual pride in that it invites the directee to approach the ministry as a contemplative exercise of taking a 'long, loving look at the real'.[2] We need to learn to develop the humility whereby we can sit before God's compassionate gaze until we can own who we are in God's sight. As St Irenaeus of Lyons famously declared way back in the second century:

> The glory of God is man [sic] fully alive;
> and the life of man is the vision of God.[3]

The struggle to integrate the different and sometimes conflicting parts of oneself forms part of the journey to holiness providing, of course, that in the end we desire to do so *ad majorem Dei gloriam* and not merely our own satisfaction. So spiritual direction invites us to own any inner movements of anger, desire, hate, lust, etc., which may not, at first, appear to concern God for they form some of those deep inner movements that are the subject of the ministry. Direction, like some therapeutic practices, addresses the whole person but differs from counselling by engaging in a process of attending to the movements of one's own 'spirits' and the Divine Spirit within us. Nor is it time limited; a directee might meet with the same director on a regular basis (every six to eight weeks) for many years. Rather, it's been likened to an Emmaus journey during which we're encouraged to become aware of the presence of Christ (some call it the ministry of 'spiritual accompaniment'). It's not the same as two friends helping each other or engaging in useful and interesting conversation, or theological or ecclesiastical discussion, nor is it an opportunity to focus on problems in the parish, difficulties with colleagues, etc., although such problems, and the feelings associated with them, may rightly be brought into direction because they provide the context and need naming. While any problems are best dealt with in supervision, the way they affect, and are affected by, the directee's relationship with God means that this material also has a place in this ministry.

For all these reasons, it's normal for ordinands and clergy to be encouraged, if not required, to have a director who will keep the eye of their heart fixed on God, something that can be easily overlooked during the demands of training and ministry.

The desire for God

I wonder if you've ever noticed that, unlike many of the Admission liturgies for Religious, those for the ordination of deacons and priests in the Church of England do not, at any point, ask that simple question: 'What do you seek?' They only ask if the person has been found to be of 'godly life and sound learning'. The notion that priests might need to *grow* in holiness isn't mentioned – that's not what ordination is all about! Is it? I've heard it suggested that this is one reason some clergy don't realize that this lies at the heart of ministry. Others have wondered if, by personality and training, some may have a well-developed 'left-brain' and need help in nurturing a more felt, intuitive realization of God. If that's you, then you might find a spirituality that involves music, fiction, poetry or art useful for God can break in through these ways which take us out of ourselves. So, for example, I've found that sitting before the Rothko murals in the Tate

Modern really helps put me in touch with my inner life. What helps you?

A *note for spiritual directors*

I wonder if you've noticed how some clergy are drawn to talk about what they're doing rather than what God might be doing with them. 'Doing' might form the context, but a director needs to avoid getting stuck at this level of engagement. While they need to meet a directee 'where they are' and listen to, often lengthy, accounts of what's happening, they also need to avoid the temptation to interrupt and ask 'and where is God in all this?' until the context has been processed. It's the kind of reflective question ministers need to be asking of themselves, and in my experience the work of the director at this point is to be watching for those signs of the Spirit at work – often she will be somewhere on the margins trying to get a look in. When I was in SSF, the wise priest-director to whom many of us went frequently waited patiently and graciously until I had finished a long account of my problems and then paused. And in that pause he was watching, I now see, for what emerged in his awareness of God working in both himself and in me.

Some will feel daunted by the prospect of directing clergy, but it should be remembered that many of them will find it as difficult to talk about their inner life as anyone else and it can take time for even a priest to talk about how God is drawing them! So remember that in helping clergy look at this, you're helping them uncover hidden riches. Directors will also need to notice what might be emerging in their own hearts' awareness as they listen – they may be the only person with whom a priest feels comfortable enough to share their deepest desires. And if the director gets irritable, let them notice that and wonder why? Don't let feelings get in the way, but if they do – and *won't* go away – they need appropriate sharing, which might be with a supervisor – or even the directee.

It's also possible that ministers will need reminding that the pastoral experiences they can't or won't let go of may reflect aspects of their own story. We should never forget that in this world of pastoral encounters the life experiences of the minister will be brought to light. Clergy are unusual in this respect; encounters which seem most painful can be illuminating and difficult memories that emerge will need particular attention. And if all this becomes overwhelming, it can be helpful to recall a priest to his or her primary vocation. The danger for the director is that they will become caught in the same material in which the minister feels trapped, and both can start to wallow; the director is to be an observer more than a rescuer.

Like everyone else, clergy will sometimes need to be invited to notice how they pray (or don't) with what is brought to direction. Are they holding on to something they need to give to God? How might they do that? And remember that director and directee are different people; what works for one won't necessarily work for the other. So asking them what might help/work etc. is really important as is the sort of question that probes just how the minister gives time to God. When did they last have a retreat, quiet day, etc. And check what happened – as necessary as they might be, pampering days at a health spa aren't quite the same as an eight-day individually guided retreat!

RETREATS AND QUIET DAYS

There's a long tradition that those seeking God will make an annual Retreat and have regular Quiet Days, a pattern which clergy especially need to attend if they're going to live a balanced life of involvement and withdrawal. For many, this will have already become an established part of their life, but if you're unsure how to go about finding a place advice can always be sought from a spiritual director or area Spirituality Adviser. The annual *Retreats Handbook* of the ecumenical Retreat Association also provides invaluable help.

Clergy who find that the pressure of life or family needs prevent them getting away even for a day need encouragement to set aside time for a retreat in everyday life through extended daily prayer times. The same would apply to Quiet Days, and my own practice has been to try and get away to a convent or Retreat House for a monthly day of reflection and prayer. But when that's not been possible then, again, a day at home not going online, answering the phone etc. but giving time to God is a necessary substitute. Again, talk to your spiritual director about these things.

৵

PASTORAL SUPERVISION

The benefit of clergy receiving pastoral supervision has already been touched on and is becoming recognized as a means of focusing on issues that emerge in working practice. Supervision isn't *just* about those practices but looks beneath the role to process what's occurring under the surface. Anxieties can develop because of the burdens they carry, and expectations (actual or perceived), both external and internal, can build up and lead some into a state of depression. The day-to-day life of a parish priest can mask deeper needs; personal relationships can become confused and boundaries blurred. Indeed, for some clergy there *are* no boundaries and the ministerial role can overwhelm personal identity. Amid such pressures self-care is often low down, if not at the bottom, of the list of 'things that should be done'. However, by ignoring their own pastoral care aren't ministers setting a bad example? Formal supervision is a clear requirement in most secular, pastoral professions, and no comparable calling leaves the requirement for self-care to the decision of its own personnel. The ministry of pastoral supervision is intended to address this need; it is a means of being accountable to ourselves, to our vocation and to God. So what might this involve? First, it is *not* spiritual accompaniment, counselling or line management. It is a

> *regular, planned intentional and boundaried space in which a practitioner skilled in supervision (the supervisor) meets with one or more other practitioners (the supervisees) to look together at their practice. ... A relationship characterized by trust, confidentiality, support and openness that gives the supervisee freedom and safety to explore the issues arising in their work. It works within a framework of spiritual/theological understanding in dialogue with the supervisee's world view and work.*[4]

Unlike mentoring, supervision has no goal other than the *pastoral* needs of the individual and complements the ministry of spiritual direction.

స్

RULE OF LIFE

A Rule, grounded in the belief that God is constantly calling us to our primal union, seeks to express our personal vocation within the context of daily life and convey how we want to live in ways that will enable a right relationship with God and creation. How we let God mould us, rather than what we *do* to get it right with God, so that we might grow into that fullness of life we proclaim. Do we practise what we preach? God looks upon us with compassion, but are we compassionate towards ourselves? Often a Rule can be overly prescriptive – a list of New Year's resolutions rather than a means whereby we seek to nurture our awareness and appreciation of God's love for us and our love for God and others. There's a difference between pious religious practices and a healthy spirituality. To quote again from the Franciscan Principles, 'The witness of life is more eloquent than that of words' (Day 22). So any Rule needs to address the *whole* person for, in the end, a Rule is for our *life*, not a formula that must be obeyed.

It will, of course, hold us to a discipline of prayerful living – how the Office, Eucharist, personal prayer, Quiet Days and Retreats figure in our life. But it also needs to identify where we can be loved – and love – and positively encourage us to create space for our selves to flourish. It will embrace all aspects of our human as well as our spiritual life; the way we use time, talents and money as well as supporting whatever best re-creates and refreshes us, be it listening to music, looking at art, taking exercise – whatever helps human flourishing. It will remind us that at times of rest a simpler form of prayer might be needed. Our spiritual director can help us with the process of developing an appropriate Rule, and there are many resources, both written and online, which address this need.

Discernment

In developing our Rule to live life in all its fullness, we need to engage in a discernment process to realize the 'personal principles' by which we're called to live. We need to reflect on the circumstances of our life, the unique personality we are, the particularities of our relationships, types of ministry, etc. and notice what gives life, meaning and purpose. Notice also what might be ignored – our use of the talents we have, including money, for the benefit of others. Then consider how all this can help develop an authentic spirituality. What practices enable us to realize God's love for ourselves? What relationships in our life need special attention? How do they reflect God's love? How does the reign of God call to us and find expression in our life? What are our particular gifts and abilities? We need to find our 'overarching narrative' from which we can develop a set of personal 'principles' by which we seek to live.

Ignatius developed 'Rules for Discernment' in the *Spiritual Exercises* for 'perceiving and knowing ... the different movements which are caused in the soul of those who are either moving towards or away from God'.[5] He explained that, as we seek to discern those inner movements, we're helped by an awareness of spiritual 'consolation' and 'desolation'. Consolation isn't about feeling better but concerns whatever moves us towards an increase in faith, hope and love. Desolation concerns the opposite. Our task is to notice the difference through a process Ignatius called the 'Discernment of Spirits', or the movements which occur deep within the soul – movements which consist of thoughts, feelings, emotions, attractions, repulsions, inclinations, imaginings, etc.[6] As we engage in that process so we begin to identify the 'norms', or 'principles', which will help us to 'choose life' in all its fullness. Here, again, the help of a spiritual director will be beneficial.

Making choices in life

Discernment is also required in many of the choices a priest must make, not least when it comes to exploring a new ministry. We *can* become blinded by the possibilities such a move might seem to offer, what ministries might open up or how it might fulfil our desires. But what matters is discerning the will of God – what might best enable God's deepening life in us. *That's* what needs to inform our choice. What matters is that our primary desire should be to follow God's will and then to entrust our choice to God, asking that God reveal to us whether or not we have made the right choice. And if, later on, we find ourselves wondering if we have, then to believe that God will use whatever we do providing that is to the Divine glory.

ॐ

THE SINGLE LIFE

Many younger clergy will be single when they're ordained and will need to develop good, healthy relationships. Life alone is hard, and many will build up defences to manage their desires, which can, sometimes, make them appear cold or distant. But loneliness, as Mother Mary Clare SLG observed,[7] differs from aloneness. I recall, some months after leaving community, a moment of great consolation when I accepted that I might never find a partner and needed to embrace aloneness rather than the desolation of loneliness.

Spiritual direction is one place where we can be open about the difficulties experienced in this matter, and no director (or confessor) should give the impression that they are shocked or surprised by what is being opened to them. There *can* be a great loneliness associated with ordained life, and the temptation to engage in inappropriate sexual relationships, for example, is sometimes overwhelming. Passion, whether spiritual or sexual, is part of being alive. There are many ways we can indulge sexual passions; sometimes fleeting, sometimes a pattern develops. While at times we just have to work against causes of sin, intimacy – whether emotional, spiritual or sexual – is a human need, and we shouldn't feel guilty when we experience times of deep desire for such intimacy. Such a desire must not be repressed but worked with, as a sculptor might work with the material given them out of which they create something of beauty. We can always offer our desires to God in prayer – tell God what we long for, according to the Divine Will – and there will be times when it will be appropriate to take all this to spiritual direction and sometimes to Confession.

The awesome journey of integration, worked out in relation to others, provides the context from which priestly spirituality emerges and helps deepen our unique being. As in silence and stillness I open more of myself to the One who would love me into being, so in solitude I can be drawn into the fullness of life.

∾

CELIBACY

In embracing aloneness, some will hear the call to celibacy, which, like the calling to chastity in marriage, is a noble one. Indeed, chastity – that faithfulness to the one to whom a person is committed – is necessary to both states of life, requiring us to give primary attention to the other be it one's partner or God. Celibacy – abstaining from marriage or sexual relations – might be, as Jesus hints, innate, forced on someone or chosen for the sake of the kingdom (Matt. 19.12). Unlike the Roman Catholic Church, where it is normally mandatory, the requirement for clerical celibacy was abolished for the Church of England in 1549 and has never been a requirement in the Protestant churches.

Anglicans and celibacy

Many do not realize that outside of the Roman Catholic Church ordained and lay men and women who feel a call to celibacy can commit themselves to the Single Consecrated Life.[8] Some will choose to live a contemplative or eremitic life, others will be involved in active priestly ministry and some who have left Religious Life continue to sense the celibate calling. Others might eventually realize celibacy in Religious Life. Viewed negatively it involves the absence of ties and any affection for one particular person, and the celibate can avoid the inevitable aloneness of their calling by substituting immense activity and involvement. The priesthood can provide many 'escapes' from the painful path of true celibacy, and any single priest must beware the temptation to overactivity. The only way of avoiding this is to develop an ever-deepening union with Jesus for this vocation involves, in some way, being 'captured by Christ'. That consecration to him who is our life needs to fascinate the person until, eventually, they realize a need to embrace celibacy. Aided by the Song of Songs – that great celebration of passionate, intimate love, which has long been associated with the desire of the soul for God – a celibate needs to recognize the totality of their desires, including the sexual, while discovering that the attraction of at-one-ness with God is greater. Both the thirteenth-century Franciscan Ramon Lull and the sixteenth-century Carmelite John of the Cross are part of a long tradition of those who have written exquisite works about this relationship between the lover and the Beloved, and this desire for union informs the vocation of celibacy.

Such celibacy does not need anything outside itself to justify itself but does invite the celibate to an affective relationship with God and, probably (for their benefit and that of others), a public commitment to such a path. The greatest service they can offer the Church is through the witness that God is so real for them that their hearts can truly be filled – and find fulfilment – through this call. They affirm that all human intimacy finds its deepest meaning and fulfilment when it is experienced as intimacy in the Heart of God.

Recently, however, some are being told to accept this state if they are to be ordained. But if it has been abolished, should it be required of lesbian and gay clergy because they are expected to provide 'higher standards of conduct' than the laity? Does that not reinforce prejudice? The ambivalence of the Church in accepting gay people does nothing to ensure that people believe it shows Christ's compassionate love. There's enormous danger in forcing people to repress their deepest desires, and the potential for damage – to both priest and those in his or her care – is great. Having sought to live this way for many years, I know that if one is not called to it then it's wrong to try to impose it on oneself or others. For while supportive associations do exist, celibacy will rarely be an easy path to follow as Michel Quoist's 'Prayer of a Priest on Sunday Night', in his book *Prayers of Life*, powerfully acknowledges.

ॐ

PARTNERS FOR LIFE

Many are fortunate in finding a partner with whom to share life, yet partners can easily feel a mere adjunct to ministry, second fiddle to God, and spirituality books that ignore the importance of human love can trivialize the Incarnation. So what place do our partners, if we have them, our friends or maybe communities play in developing our life in Christ? While we might sense an unhealthy dualism (partner vs God), we need to remember that the fundamental attitude of the *I* to the *Thou* is to be reflected and realized in every relationship in which we engage.

Our call to be Christ's lovers and heralds of his reign will, therefore, be primarily mediated through those to whom we are committed. These loves – for Christ and my heart's delight – are not in competition but can be mutually enhancing when

I discover the love I realize in Christ flooding with light the one who Christ has given me *to* love. And I find that so liberating, for no longer do I need to compartmentalize my loving! Each of us, especially while during formation, needs to work out how those we love are part of our life in Christ and listen and support them as we trust they listen to and support us. Our love for and commitment to them will act as a reflection of our love for him whose compassionate Heart draws us, and we must beware should that love begins to tarnish or crack.

Committed love lies at the heart of our Faith and the Church lauds the state of matrimony, seeing its profound effect on our relationship with each other and God. However, if it does not allow gay or lesbian clergy to make such a commitment, it places many in a catch-22 situation by asserting that while it accepts them and rejoices in sexual intimacy, such intimacy can only be expressed within marriage. Ergo ... Many ignore this instruction and some wrestle with it, but one wonders whether this teaching best enables that fullness of life which we believe the gospel proclaims and which those who are ordained need to know is possible for them to enjoy.

∂°

PARTICULAR RELATIONSHIPS

I know just how hard loneliness can be and, consequently, realize how easy it is for clergy, and not just those who are single, to seek to alleviate or avoid aspects of it by developing close relationships with members of a congregation. Clearly, it's important to offer and receive friendship and some friendships will arise naturally; we need to be loved for who we are and not just for what we do. But jealousy can arise or factions develop and, if maintained after leaving a parish, there's always the danger of the priest becoming a type of éminence grise. This is something that could usefully be brought to spiritual direction, but I do find myself wondering if it's better to become a friend for *all* those in one's care rather than developing particular friendships? To notice the love we *do* receive, even if it doesn't come in ways we might want. As someone reminded me just before I moved into my parish: 'If you love them, they'll love you.' I vividly recall the time when, feeling my parents didn't love me, my Novice Guardian told me to go home and just notice the ways they did – it might not be how I wanted them to, but it would be the way they could. The consequent weekend was one of the most formative encounters in my life, and I've sometimes suggested to directees that they might benefit from doing something similar. We all need to know we're special to someone and, while we know we're loved by God, 'you can't hug the Blessed Sacrament' as a fellow novice once said to me.

࿇

HEALTHY LIVING

While the 'grace and power of God' is crucial if we're to bear the weight of our calling, the Ordinal doesn't say what we need to sustain that ministry in its day-to-day demands, what checks and balances we need in order to lead a healthy life in the full sense of that word. Whether by circumstance, inclination or a toxic mix of the two, some of us find ourselves more Marthas than Marys, and although we may *recognize* the importance of stepping aside from the demands of our ministry it can be easier said than done, especially if we're extraverts. The temptation to want to 'fix' everything can be great, but we're not messiahs, though some of us have a deep desire to rescue others and need to be aware of and not be driven by that complex.

As a Franciscan, I was constantly reminded that our common life was the primary place where the love of God was to be known and expressed. For those who are married or in a partnership, our families will provide that primary place; those who are celibate or single will need to develop life-giving, supportive and mutually reciprocal relationships outside the context of ministry – and does it have to be with Christians? Whatever our situation in life, we all need to realize and value the ways in which we can be known and loved – where we can face the truth of who we are in the compassionate gaze of others.

Many of us would also benefit from belonging to one of the priestly societies which exist for nurturing our *vocation* and not just our ministry, and some are fortunate to belong to a supportive Cell Group.

෨

THROUGH DARKNESS AND PERPLEXITY

Living in ordinary time means accepting grief as well as joy, pain as well as pleasure. Sometimes work just piles up and it can seem as if one is drowning. At times like this, take a deep breath! Remember, you're not the messiah, even if people want you to be. And if you have that temperament, don't forget what Jesus *said* to Martha! So after taking a deep breath, might it help to laugh at yourself? But if the darkness is overwhelming, who do you need to share the load with? After all, the cure priests receive from their bishop is not just theirs to carry, and none of us should be ashamed when it becomes too heavy for us to bear.

The joy of living out of Christ's priesthood can also be affected by times of spiritual listlessness, of *acedia* – laziness, apathy and joylessness in our prayer and wider lives – that can lead to a sense of depression. We can find ourselves wondering whether another place, parish or way of life would be more satisfying, or we can want to spend more time with *that* person. This was first realized by the Desert Fathers and Mothers who called it the work of the *noonday devil* (Ps. 91.6). At times, it afflicts everyone and is best countered by remaining faithful to our work and prayer and turning from that demon who would lead us astray. In his book *Abandonment to Divine Providence*, Jean-Pierre de Caussade SJ reminds us not to allow such times to overcome us while realizing the importance *of* such times: 'God instructs the heart, not by ideas but by pains and contradictions.' He goes on to develop the Ignatian principle that, at such times, we should not make any sudden changes or seek for distractions but trust in Divine providence until we pull through.

I've also found the simple advice of two great nuns helpful. First, Dame Laurentia McLachlan OSB who, on being elected Abbess of Stanbrook in 1931, said: 'I can't; you must', and when going through a difficult time – physically and spiritually – Mother Jane Margaret CSMV simply observed in her diary: 'Pull on, old ox.' Both these avowals are a reminder of the teaching of Ignatius that we should always 'act against' (*agere contra*) that which is causing feelings of desolation or joylessness. To fix the gaze of our heart more profoundly on that which is life-giving, on the Heart of Jesus. And take all this to spiritual direction. As one Sister of the Love of God wrote concerning times of great difficulty:

> *What GOD is concerned to give is not <u>alleviation</u> but the <u>power to go on enduring</u> – to pass through distress and still remain constant – to transcend, to rise above and beyond things so hard to the natural self. To <u>transcend</u> depends on <u>our will and His Gift</u> – Our task to let His Will and His Life live in us. We rise above things just in proportion as He lives our life. There is a wonderful clearing of the spiritual sight – the opening out of a whole*

*new world of understanding and confidence for the soul
that can trust itself wholly to Our Lord.*

———

*Why are you cast down, my soul,
why groan within me?
Hope in God; I will praise him yet again,
my saving presence and my God.
(Psalm 43.5 from the traditional
Prayers of Preparation before Mass)*

Our life will include times of darkness and perplexity. The
priest needs to set this in the context of sharing in the Passion
of Christ else it may be a burden too heavy to bear: 'lead us
not into temptation'. It can make all the difference, for the
door into his sorrow is also the door into his joy.

Growing into Christ

Growing into Christ is an evolutionary process. Please God,
our priesthood will mature as we do and what we might
have perceived daunting at one time will prove less so as we
grow. Hopefully we will experience a desire to give more
time to prayer. Some will realize a need to join a priestly
association, dispersed religious congregation or Religious
Life itself. Others may find that a particular spirituality
draws them and feel called to life as an oblate or tertiary
of an established Religious congregation. This can help us
grow as we become more confident in our-'self' and recognize who is the 'me' that's living my life (*'my me is Christ
...'*). Inevitably, we will experience times of darkness and
confusion when God seems far away, inspiration elusive and
life hard. It's at such times that the help of a director will
be of immense value, although what is most important (and
difficult) is that we stick to what has been life-giving and

pray through it for such periods will probably, in the end, be realized as times of great growth. Out of chaos comes the shooting star.

Jesus, I trust in your mercy.

Questions for reflection

- Do I need to find a spiritual director? A pastoral supervisor?
- Where do my passions – my desires – lie? Do I desire to love God with my whole heart and my neighbour as myself? Is this something I could take to spiritual direction? Is there anything I might need to take to Confession or supervision?
- How far do my moods to determine how I live? Again, is this something I should take to direction?
- *(For celibates)* Is my celibacy chosen, embraced, grudgingly accepted or resented? How can it become life-giving?

Notes

1 By kind permission of James Keegan SJ, *Presence* (magazine of Spiritual Directors International. Edition not found).

2 Walter Burghardt, SJ, 'Contemplation: A Long Loving Look at the Real', in *An Ignatian Spirituality Reader*, ed. W. Traub, Loyola Press, 2008.

3 St Irenaeus of Lyons (c. AD 180), *Against Heresies*, Book 4, 20.7.

4 Definition of Supervision by the Association for Pastoral Supervision and Education (APSE).

5 *Spiritual Exercises*, paras 313–36.

6 There are many good books on Ignatian discernment one of which, *Sleeping with Bread* (Paulist Press, 1995), also deals with the Examen.

7 Mother Mary Clare SLG, 2010, *Aloneness not Loneliness*, revised edition, SLG Press, 2010.

8 A 'Fresh Expression' of the monastic life. (http://www.singleconsecratedlife-anglican.org.uk).

9

Being Beneath the Role

Discovering our personal vocation

࿇

*Will you endeavour to fashion your own life and that
of your household according to the way of Christ, that
you may be a pattern and example to Christ's people?
(Ordination of Priests: The Declarations)*

'What a piece of work is a man!'

Forgive the gender-specific noun, but I'm only quoting Shake-
speare as Hamlet ruminates on his plight with his old friends,
Rosencrantz and Guildenstern. He goes on to observe:

*How noble in reason, how infinite in faculty! In form and
moving how express and admirable! In action how like
an angel! In apprehension how like a god! The beauty of
the world! The paragon of animals! And yet to me, what
is this quintessence of dust?*[1]

This chapter is concerned with looking behind the 'express
and admirable' aspect of our role to who, beneath it, we
are. I've noticed how easy it is, over time, for clergy to begin
losing touch with their personal identity as they live out of
their role, and while the mantle of Elijah helped Elisha in his
prophetic ministry, Elisha maintained his own identity as he
lived out his calling.

When I began life as a Franciscan I wanted to be the best friar I could be, so I wore the habit as often as possible until I realized, of course, that the habit doesn't make the monk (or friar) even though it can help form him. We know that the task of priestly formation isn't so much about becoming something different but becoming more fully who we are as we allow Christ's priesthood to inhabit us. But it's always the unique 'me' that's to be clothed in Christ and we need to relish and celebrate our own 'piece of work'.

అ

THE PARADOX OF BEING

The invitation to 'be yourself' has become axiomatic: 'Be yourself', declared Oscar Wilde, 'everyone else is already taken.' That advice can be offered in a kindly or challenging way so when early in my Franciscan life a brother suddenly blurted out: 'Oh, for goodness sake, be yourself!' I became rather confused and angry; wasn't I supposed to be dying to myself? But I'm grateful for the card he later gave me, which contained these words by Paul Tillich:

> *The courage to be*
> *is the ethical act*
> *in which man affirms his own being*
> *in spite of those elements of his existence*
> *which conflict with his essential*
> *self-affirmation.*[2]

That tortuous piece of philosophy echoed in me, and I often quietly repeated it, allowing the words to sink into my soul. What, exactly, did they mean for me? I thought I had 'been' and was on the road to 'becoming', had let go of my old self and put on the new man. I didn't want to be the person

I had been and thought I could put him aside. After all, didn't Jesus say, 'If any want to become my followers, let them deny themselves and take up their cross and follow me' (Matt. 16.24)? And here I was, taking up my cross, denying myself (not least sexually) and following him. Wasn't I called to stop 'being myself'? But Tillich's words eventually helped me realize the necessity of living with and through paradox, something Jesus wonderfully captured as he went on to say:

> *(for) those who want to save their life will lose it, and those who lose their life for my sake will find it. For what will it profit them if they gain the whole world but forfeit their life? Or what will they give in return for their life? (Matthew 16.25f.)*

Isn't there always a tussle between the two, the 'letting go' and the 'owning' of self? Charles Williams, the theologian-poet, pointed to this when he wrote of the nature of God: 'This Also Is Thou; Neither Is This Thou.'[3] It's a reflection of the fact that God can be known (immanent) and yet remains unknown (transcendent), the paradox of weeds that must grow among the wheat, of sheep and goats living together. We'll always exist in that paradox until we come to face the One in whose image we are made and in which we are formed by the interweaving of his and our dying and rising; the paradox we celebrate in the *Exsultet* as the Paschal Candle is lit early on Easter Day:

> *O happy fault, O necessary sin of Adam,*
> *which gained for us so great a Redeemer!*

Putting on masks

It's no wonder, then, that some give in to the temptation to wear a mask as they worry about what others think of them (what the bishop might think of them). Yet it's often not the present person they're seeking to satisfy but one from the long-distant past – a parent or teacher – until they find themselves going down that slippery slope towards living a false life where they appear one thing but, in the darkness, are driven by another. Have you ever considered that your 'role-self' (vicar, archdeacon, chaplain, etc.) might be dominating who you are? As difficult as it may be, it's important to take care not to act out of a role but to be honest about ourselves and seek to be authentic and brave and not pretend to be something we're not – especially if this involves, which it can, wanting to please people.

> *O LORD, you search me and you know me.*
> *You yourself know my resting and my rising;*
> *you discern my thoughts from afar ...*
> *you know all my ways through and through ...*
> *O where can I go from your spirit,*
> *or where can I flee from your face?*
> *(Psalm 139.1, 2, 3, 7)*

If we start ministry in our youth, this 'putting on the role' or developing a 'persona' as Jung noticed can be almost inevitable, especially if there's a priest on whom we want to model ourselves. There's nothing wrong with wanting to emulate a good, holy priest just as long as we remember they lived out of their unique holiness and we need to live out of ours. What God has created is perfect in his sight – in need of redemption, yes, but intrinsically perfect – *for that is the person God has called to the priesthood.* In seeking to live a holy life, we must beware the monstrous voice of perfectionism which can overwhelm the love and passion connected with who and what we truly are.

Engulfed by Church

While it's not a mask, I've noticed that there's another way that we can lose ourselves and that concerns the way the Church can sometimes be overwhelming. I don't just mean the way in which the boundary between work and life can be unclear but also the way in which clergy can become overwhelmed by the dynamics which emerge in the life of a church. This happens in every workplace ('they're ganging up on me', 'how can I be acceptable?', 'there's so much they expect me to do'...) but, because that work–life boundary can be fluid for clergy, a priest needs to recognize what's happening and find ways of extracting themselves. If we're submerged by negative dynamics not only can they be a cause for desolation but they'll affect the way we relate with ourselves and others. This is material for supervision and, at times, spiritual direction for as Christ descended into the grave to liberate the imprisoned souls (1 Peter 3.18f.) so he seeks to enter our inner darkness to set us free.

Spirituality and sexuality

One of the great paradoxes of faith is the way these two concepts are so closely allied. Many years ago, I was fortunate to be able to spend time in Spain exploring something of the spirituality of Teresa of Avila and John of the Cross. It was at a time when I was struggling with the pulls of sexuality and spirituality and I recall the shock I experienced on encountering a painting of the 'Transverberation of St Teresa', which shows her heart being pierced by long dart 'to her very entrails' as commentators say. I suddenly found that what had seemed opposing were, actually, closely related and on returning to London began to reflect more deeply on this:

Abandonment to desire
Letting go
Exploration
Dart of longing love
Breaking of barriers
Entering the mystery
Gift of self
Totality of freedom
Explosion of creative energy
Orgasm ... prayer ...
Insurge of love
Being at one
Perfection of joy
Exquisiteness of pain
Openness to the Spirit
Yearning for the other
Gift of adoration
Desire of the heart
Whoever loves is born of God and knows God ...

Christianity proclaims this blissful union with God, not absorption into God, and many spiritual writers share the realization that, in our desire for union, spirituality is the close ally of sensuality. More recently Alice Walker, in *The Color Purple*, wrote of the way Shug tries to help Celie get past her image of God as 'an old white man' advocating a more 'God in all things' approach. Finally, laughing aloud, she rubs her hand high on her thigh declaring that God 'loves all those feelings' and that when you know God loves them 'you enjoys 'em a whole lot more'.

Can we delight in our sexuality and allow it to express our desire for God? If we can, then it might enable a powerful rediscovery of our desire to be given wholly to the Other.

❧

BEING HONEST

Sadly, the temptation to deny aspects of our identity can be strong. Some feel ashamed at what they've done or what has happened to them in life and long to be free of that feeling. Others will need to acknowledge that they are trapped by addiction, whatever its form, while others battle depression or simply don't feel 'good enough'. It can be painful to be reconciled to the truth of who we are or what has happened in our life, hard to be honest about this and to have the humility to accept the awful fact that beneath what people see there's another reality. All this is material which needs to be brought to spiritual direction because, whatever the cause which may need dealing with in therapy, a deep spiritual malaise can also be present.

Times of crisis can occur when the hidden cries out for attention, times which can be opportunities for real growth and development. But growth isn't *dependent* on crisis if we have the humility and courage to own what's denied and open it to the compassionate gaze of God. This terrible but vital invitation to be real is offered to everyone yet can be hard to accept when we fear doing so will cause us to be rejected. This can be true for all Christians but especially for clergy due to the expectations placed on them, and while we can avoid the path to 'being real' it is one not even clergy can escape. I still recall the time during a mission when I was asked to meet with a young curate from a nearby parish who was beginning to accept that he was gay but feared his Church, which taught that homosexuality was sinful, finding out. I was later told he committed suicide.

࿐

BEING DIFFERENT: LGBTI

One of the greatest challenges for some is that struggle with issues concerning sexuality, which, while not specific to the clergy, can be a particular problem. In a Church where many still reject those who are gay ('practising homosexuals'), seek to convert them, cast out the demon of homosexuality or pray them into heterosexuality, no wonder there are so many who feel forced to hide or deny fundamental aspects of their identity. Sadly, the abusive behaviour of some clergy – whether it be spiritual, emotional or theological (especially if they 'run successful parishes') – is often left unchallenged. Those of us who are LGBTI may feel a need to hide our basic identity – something that can be quite easy to do, in order to be 'acceptable' – but we are in danger, like Archbishop Cranmer, of carrying our metaphorical wife around in a coffin.

This book can only acknowledge that our sexual identity is of immense importance to every aspect of our life – something to be relished, not ashamed of – and one can only hope that those in authority will at least exercise acceptance and empathy towards those who are LGBTI. Some of us are fortunate to have parishes and bishops who do that and value us because of who we are. I still recall the two elderly ladies, not Anglicans, who came up to me in the street shortly after my civil partnership to congratulate me and wish us well.

Sadly, some clergy may feel the need to repress, rather than suppress, their feelings, which can lead to situations when that which is denied or locked away can emerge in unhealthy or risky behaviour. The suppression of desires can be positive, but their repression can be dangerous. It's often only after a long, painful, confusing and sometimes chaotic struggle, where issues of shame and guilt are faced, that we can come to terms with our identity (if we do), and in that messy process there can be a lot of collateral damage. All this needs to be the subject of our prayer (asking for enlightenment and grace, not for the burden to be removed) and self-acceptance as well as the help of a wise director and, when necessary, therapist.

࿇

BEING IN CHRIST

All this 'being and becoming' can be swallowed up in the multiplicity of tasks and expectations placed upon priests, as well as expectations we can have of ourselves, until doing takes over from being. That long list of what priests are called to do in the 'Declarations' at ordination can drown the poor priest beneath an ever-increasing deluge of responsibilities. And when that happens, it's helpful to recall that the most important thing we can do is to give it all to God. There's a wonderful line in the *Rule for a New Brother* which simply reminds us that in Jesus we see how one person can completely belong to God and how much 'freedom and humanity' can be found when one is surrendered to him.

To surrender myself to him! Each morning we might make that part of our prayer: 'Father, today I abandon myself into your hands: do with me what you will.' Our being for his glory! We should never forget the immense riches we possess in Christ through whom we are sanctified. 'O Christian, learn to appreciate your dignity', exclaimed St Leo.[4] Might not priests, especially, need to meditate on that invitation? For it is from our being a beloved child of the God who has adopted us that priestly life flows.

Beneath the role

While this desire for union with Christ is at the heart of our calling, I've noticed, in directing clergy, that many find it easier to talk about roles and responsibilities. Although ministry may form the expression of our vocation, it's not its essence, for that can only be found as *Cor ad cor loquitur* – 'Heart speaks to heart'.[5] Vocation concerns the heart of being which our actions express. The demands of ministry can overbalance the call to intimacy and relationship just as doing can easily replace being in our desire for meaning. And while this isn't unique to priesthood, unless our vocation is rooted in the desire for union with Christ, sooner or later it will wither – and may die.

Many find the life of the Curé d'Ars or the nineteenth-century 'slum priests' to be inspirational and, more recently, some of Michel Quoist's *Prayers of Life* speak into the priestly life. However, I wonder if part of the difficulty around the matter of developing a healthy spirituality arises because much that has been written has come from the pens of celibates. A healthy spirituality needs to take into account our primary relational calling. Whether a priest is celibate, partnered or single, the essence of holiness is tested through human relationships and a growing realization that, although we are wounded and broken, we are loved to the depth of our being.

Love is the kingdom which the Lord mystically promised to the disciples. (St Isaac the Syrian)

The call to sanctity

Sometimes we encounter a person so outrageously themselves that it shocks us. At such moments, it may be our false inner self that's being shocked. We glimpse the possibility of a life that can be lived to the full, with all our creative energies flowing, yet fear holds us back. I've made many mistakes in my life having sinned in thought, word and deed; failed in this call to accept who God is lovingly creating me to be – but

I have longed to carry on the journey of self-discovery as I have listened to the invitation to 'be myself'. Merton teaches that this call is the way to sanctity for the 'real' or 'true' self emerges from the struggle towards living out the truth of who we are before God.[6] So we need to engage in a constant finding and letting go of self, a gifting of self and being utterly present to the Other. What a calling for the priest! Our vocation is not simply to 'be' but to co-operate with God in this matter of our ongoing co-creation, the creation of our own identity which will involve a process of self-abandonment.

This call also challenges us to reflect on Jesus' summons to give ourselves to the kingdom. In the Second Week of the *Exercises*, Ignatius encourages us to relate to Christ from that perspective. Apart from considering the need for humility and indifference, he asks his retreatants to 'choose poverty with Christ' rather than riches. While we may not hear that specific call, priests need to reflect on the way the style and manner of our lives reflects the gospel. The call to holiness has always involved the invitation to abandon everything for Christ, and we need to ponder what our lives say about our desires.

❧

THE PERSONAL VOCATION

If you get a bit lost in this call and find it difficult to express your relationship with Christ apart from your role, don't forget the importance of rediscovering your primary vocation. What was it that drew you to this expression of the love of the Heart of Jesus? What attracted you to him and what about him did you want to express? Was there a word you heard in your heart to which you desired to give expression? Remembering that can bring us back to our personal vocation. We might get excited about what we're doing, but it's more important to dig a little deeper and realize just what led, moved, urged us to give *this* expression of God's continuing call that is heard echoing – maybe dimly – in the heart. What is the 'name' you heard God call? Many instances in the Bible refer to this 'called by name' from the prophecy of Isaiah (43.1) to our new name written on stone known only to the one who receives it (Rev. 2.17). And in all this, the call of Abram who became Abraham (Gen. 17.5) is fundamental for, like him, to realize our true identity will require leaving the known for the unknown.

In his book *Discovering Your Personal Vocation*, Herbert Alphonso explores how God calls each of us by a hidden name that describes who we are. That 'name' is an expression of our 'true self' and describes our personal vocation, something we realize as we journey with the Lord and, when we do so, know that *thi*s is our calling. While giving life and meaning to our ministerial vocation, it is far deeper than that. For example, our personal vocation might be 'Good Shepherd'; 'sufferings of Christ'; 'compassionate companion'. From this core-self our vocation emerges.

It was once common for religious to take a personal dedication, for example 'of the Cross', 'of the Holy Child', etc., all of which express a sense of a particular calling. St Francis found his when, according to *The Legend of the Three Companions*,[7] he heard God say: 'Francis, if you want to know my will, you will have to hate and detest everything which, until this moment, you have loved and longed to make your own.' Thus he betrothed himself to Lady Poverty, his personal vocation. Alphonso maintains that one finds an inner freedom through discovering this call, which allows each person to realize their truest self and become, within the Body, the unique person God intends them to be. This transformation in depth is akin to the Ignatian 'Election' – the realization of what God is calling us to in life – which lies at the heart of the *Spiritual Exercises*.

Letting go

This journey into being can sometimes cause a priest to face the dreadful dilemma that the structural Church is preventing their deepest vocation. There is no doubt that, in all its earthly manifestations, the Church is flawed, and many looking at her will only see the rags of prejudice, rejection and hypocrisy with which Christ has been clothed. Some come to a point when they feel the need to cast aside those garments in order to be true to their personal rather than ecclesial vocation. This is a tremendous step into the unknown and one of the most difficult discernments for a priest to make, and it needs the help of an experienced director. But, if the person makes that step with the Lord, they will, in the end, be safe.

> *Though I should walk in the valley*
> *of the shadow of death,*
> *no evil would I fear,*
> *for you are with me.*
> *Your crook and your staff*
> *will give me comfort.*
> *(Psalm 23.4)*

Questions for reflection

- What gives meaning and life to *your* vocation? What was it about Jesus that attracted you?
- How might you express your 'personal vocation'? What is your deepest desire?
- How does the gospel challenge your style and manner of life?

Notes

1 *Hamlet*, Act II, Scene 2.
2 Paul Tillich, *The Courage to Be*, 2nd edn, Yale University Press, 2000.
3 Charles Williams and C. S. Lewis, *Taliessin Through Logres, The Region of the Summer Stars, and Arthurian Torso*, Eerdmans, 1974, p. 335.
4 St Leo the Great, 'Sermo 22 in nat. Dom.', 3, in *Patrologia Latina* 54, 192C.
5 Motto of Bl. John Henry Newman from a letter of St Francis de Sales to a directee.
6 Thomas Merton, *Seeds of Contemplation*, New Direction, 1987, p. 47.
7 *Legend of the Three Companions*, ch. 4.11.

10

In My End is My Beginning

Life in the Trinity

჻

There's a statue of Our Lady in the chapel of the (Anglican) Poor Clares at Freeland, near Oxford, which portrays a gently smiling Mary holding out her child to the world. He, in turn, reaches out his arms to whoever stands before him. It's a statue that has always spoken powerfully to me of the way Jesus wants us to take him into our hearts as he, in turn, is taking us into him in whom we long to abide (John 15).

Throughout this book reference has been made to the *Spiritual Exercises*, which can either be undertaken during a 30-day retreat or in the context of a retreat in daily life. In the final Week of these, Ignatius invites those undertaking them to an intimate knowledge of the way God, in his love, shares all that he is with us that we might share all we are with him. He offers retreatants a final 'Contemplation on the Love of God', which invites them to consider God's limitless love and to make a generous response of love in return. Endings can be hard, even when we're looking forward to something else; concerns about what we have and have not done – the omissions and commissions of life – can obstruct the gift of ourselves into this new phase of life in Christ, so this final chapter is set in the context of that final invitation into the love of God.

Retiring?

I'm often asked, in a kindly way, if I'm enjoying my 'retire-ment', and immediately conjure up a picture of armchairs, pipes and slippers, afternoons playing golf and cruises in the Mediterranean. Isn't that what retirement involves? Although we might lay our role aside, can we *ever* retire from our voca-tion, from being who we are? When do we reach the moment we can say, 'It is accomplished'?

In attempting to explore what lies behind the outer expres-sions of the priesthood, I've come to the time when priests need to consider letting go of their responsibilities and roles. It's one of the most difficult shifts in life as it probably involves us in facing a period of a real and deep sense of bereavement, a time that's easy to fill with a host of other things that can distract us from fully entering this new stage of our calling when we stand at the threshold of what we have celebrated in every Eucharist. Instead of lamenting how little time we have for prayer, we can now have too much time at our disposal! It can take years to emerge out of this period as we seek to realize afresh our personal vocation and find new ways in which it can be expressed. Yet, freed from the demands of any role, this is the time when we can reconsider how to live out of Jesus' compassionate Heart for the world.

&

LOVE WAS OUR LORD'S MEANING

This book has tried to show that what matters is not just what we do but the way that we do it so that we can join Dag Hammarskjöld in saying, 'For all that has been, thanks. For all that will be, yes!'[1] In the end, our 'yes' must be to the desire to dwell in that City which embraces people 'from every nation, from all tribes and peoples and languages' (Rev.

7.9). One of the greatest tasks of those who preach the Faith of Christ crucified is to remind our sisters and brothers that we are, ultimately, called out of any existential loneliness into being enfolded in the Trinity. In his great work, *De Trinitate*, Augustine declares:

> *Love, therefore, which is of God and is God, is specially the Holy Spirit, by whom the love of God is shed abroad in our hearts, by which love the whole Trinity dwells in us.*[2]

And Bernard of Clairvaux expresses that life in this deeply intimate way:

> *If ... the Father is he who kisses, the Son he who is kissed, then it cannot be wrong to see in the kiss the Holy Spirit, for he is the imperturbable peace of the Father and the Son, their unshakable bond, their undivided love, their indivisible unity.*[3]

Christianity proclaims a blissful union with, not absorption into, God for

> *we shall rest and we shall see; we shall see and we shall love; we shall love and we shall praise. Behold what shall be in the end and shall not end.*[4]

I am in Christ and Christ enfolds me, transfigures the darkness of my heart. It is a time when we can become old and crotchety or transparent with love ...![5]

> *There is one thing I ask of the Lord, for this I long,*
> *to live in the house of the Lord, all the days of my life,*
> *to savour the sweetness of the Lord,*
> *to behold his temple.*
> *(Psalm 27.4)*

IN MY END IS MY BEGINNING

In my end is my beginning

Those words, familiar to lovers of T. S. Eliot's poetry, originate from Mary, Queen of Scots towards the end of her life. When we come to leave our roles, we mustn't cease exploring, mustn't cease desiring to deepen the calling we've received. In a way, we become freer to be penetrated *by* that love that calls us. As we get older, perhaps we need to recall how St Bernard went on to say:

> *In the first creation He gave me myself; but in His new creation He gave me Himself, and by that gift restored to me the self that I had lost. Created first and then restored, I owe Him myself twice over in return for myself. But what have I to offer Him for the gift of Himself? Could I multiply myself a thousand-fold and then give Him all, what would that be in comparison with God.*[6]

Like George Herbert and Ignatius of Loyola, we're called to let Jesus flow into who we are and to allow who we are to be clothed in him. That co-mingling performed by the priest at the Offertory as water is poured into wine symbolizes how our humanity is to be taken into his Divinity as we continue to allow ourselves to be changed by God's desire for at-oneness with us 'from glory to glory'. However our priesthood is expressed, we're called to live intensely, to be set apart in him and never cease believing 'that we are consecrated to give our wills to Jesus, and in giving our wills to lay ourselves body and soul in his hands that he may do what he will with us'.[7]

Indifference

Throughout our ministry, we commit ourselves to many places and people in a unique way. We've noticed how that commitment can cause problems as we go on unless we also develop what Ignatius called in his *Exercises* a spirit of 'indifference',[8] a certain freedom or detachment 'from the things of this world' that might prevent us from attaining the end we seek – union in the love of God. He goes on to write of the way we need to develop that spirit in order to choose what is most consistent with the will of God:

> *I should be like a balance at equilibrium without leaning to either side, that I might be ready to follow whatever I perceive is more for the glory and praise of God our Lord and for the salvation of my soul.*[9]

I'm grateful to Ignatius for many things but not least for reminding me that my one desire and choice must be whatever leads to God's life being deepened in me.

❧

LETTING GO

Throughout life, 'letting go' will have been an underlying motif. Now it takes on a new reality as we have to let go of so much that has given our life meaning and purpose. It always takes courage to let go, and to let go of *those* things requires even more and can be really hard if we've not been practising letting go before now. The consideration 'who am I now I have no role?', or 'how can I exercise my vocation now I don't have a role?' can be of deep concern.

To the glory of God

So as we look towards the moment when we shall stand before a beginning that has no end, we're invited into that 'thin place' of heaven's in-breaking. Behind whatever expression of the priesthood we may have exercised, in the end it's all about giving glory to God. About consecrating our lives to him until, please God, we become fully united in God. We are to let go of all the contexts behind our ministries – the loves and loneliness, successes and failures, intense relationships, broken dreams and all the rest – and realize that all we're required to do is to try our best and leave the rest to God.

> *Do not remember the sins of my youth,*
> *nor my transgressions.*
> *In your merciful love remember me,*
> *because of your goodness, O Lord.*
> *(Psalm 25.7)*

If you look back and, wondering at the meaning of it all, are tempted to despair, recall that what you did was for the glory of God. And, where it wasn't, seek forgiveness. And if you look back at what came into being through your ministry which later fell into ruins or lament what you didn't achieve, then grieve and mourn by all means, but the past is behind you and that, too, needs to be given away. Live in the present moment. It's so easy to waste time dwelling in the past, or worrying about an uncertain future, and never be living in this moment given us by God because, of course, there's no other in which we can *live*.

Abandoned to love

Yes, old age can bring bitterness over the past, anger felt and hurts never healed. Shortly after I founded the Spiritual Association CHJM, someone wrote to me:

> *I've noticed that, as some people get older, they become increasingly bitter and resentful about what life hurls at them. They may even choose to have hatred running in their lives. It sort of energizes them and keeps them going.*

So we must avoid bitterness and remember that the action performed hundreds of times in the Eucharist is now one which invites us to raise hands, eyes and hearts to God that we might become a living sacrifice, wholly acceptable to God (Rom. 12.1). Death invites us into that final abandonment into the eternal ocean of love when it is by our loving we'll be judged.

> Lord of the faithful, guide us on our journey:
> Pilgrims, we hunger for the life of heaven.
> Jesus, our manna, feed us with your goodness
> Here and hereafter.[10]

As we grow older, we need to remember that what can't be taken from us is our vocation to union with the Divine. No one can take away our desire to live out of the Divine Will: 'thy will be done' in me and all your Creation. Our spirituality is both an expression and means of developing that calling which is now into the priesthood of waiting as we realize new ways to love with the Heart of Jesus. We've been the best priest we can be – now we're invited into the spaciousness of his loving Heart.

༄

ATTAINING THE LOVE OF GOD

In concluding his *Exercises* with that final 'Contemplation', Ignatius reminds us that love ought to show itself in deeds more than words and invites us to remember that true love seeks to share all with the beloved. Love, then, becomes our meaning and there is no place it cannot be realized. Our altar becomes the world and creation the elements of our loving celebration. God has given us all things – now we begin to return them. This is the final duet between the soul and God until God embraces us into himself. Life has invited us to embark on a pilgrimage of integration worked out in relation to others and nurtured in silence and stillness. As we open more of ourselves to God ('I offer you my soul and body to be a living sacrifice') who would love us into being, we recognize what draws us more deeply into life. Priestly spirituality, rooted in humility, realizes the call all have to divinity as we desire, moment by moment, to live with faith, hope and love that we might truly become that *alter Christus*. Whatever we might do after we've laid down our cure, it is love that is to remain. We might then notice that something quite different is drawing us – volunteering in a school, helping out in a social project, developing a ministry that beforehand was peripheral. And all the time, that invitation: 'It is no longer I who live, but it is Christ who lives in me. And the life I now live in the flesh I live by faith in the Son of God, who loved me and gave himself for me.' (Gal. 2.20)

> *Love is not changed by Death,*
> *And nothing is lost*
> *And all in the end is harvest.*[11]

All in the end is harvest

As we look forward to death, we recognize it as but a movement into eternal life begun at our baptism into Christ when 'we are clothed with Christ, dying to sin that we may live the risen life.'[12] By the grace of God, we've been growing into Christ, growing into the priestly garments with which we're clothed, seeking to become that which we proclaim. Discovering the 'priest within'. In the Roman Catholic Rite of Baptism there's a short ceremony towards the end when the ears and mouth of the neophyte are touched and the 'Ephphatha Prayer' offered over them, which asks that the one who made the deaf hear and the dumb speak may touch their ears to hear God's word and open their mouth to proclaim his faith to the praise and glory of God. The rest of life, especially the life of those ordained to preside over the Mysteries of the Kingdom, concerns this 'opening of the ears of the heart' to the word of the Lord. Ambrose of Milan said that we are to open our ears and take the sweetness of eternal life which has been breathed on us by the gift of baptism.[13] May our ears be always open to that Word! As the 'Principles' of the Spiritual Association of the Compassionate Hearts of Jesus and Mary say:

> *Finally Companions, like all Christians, are called to a constant conversion of their hearts until they reflect the glory of God in whose image and likeness they are made. We must seek first the kingdom of God and his righteousness (Matthew 6.33) for where our treasure lies, there will our hearts be also. (Matthew 6.21)*

This, of course, must also be true for priests. Just as St Francis described himself as a 'herald of the Great King', so we're called to proclaim, in all we do and say, the Christ who is the inspiration and joy of our own lives. We're called to make of the whole of life a prayer by inclining our heart to the Heart of him who seeks to enfold us. We're called to witness to that love and remember, as Julian of Norwich said, how much we are loved, for when our ministry is ended this remains: 'the priesthood is the love of the heart of Jesus'.

> *Glory be to the Father,*
> *and to the Son,*
> *and to the Holy Spirit;*
> *As it was in the beginning,*
> *is now and ever shall be,*
> *world without end. Amen.*

✠

Final questions for reflection

- Spend time reflecting on God's love for you. Write down/
draw your response. Is there anything you notice? What is
it saying to you?
- Recall how your life has been/is being blessed. Recall all the
gifts and graces you have received. For what do you especially wish to give thanks?
- What aspect of Jesus' life, passion and death speaks most
powerfully to you? What is that saying to you, now, in relation to your ministry?
- Write your own epitaph; what do you want to celebrate and
give thanks for?

Notes

1 Dag Hammarskjöld, *Markings*, Ballantine, 1983 [1964], p. 74.
2 Augustine, *De Trinitate*, 15.32.
3 Bernard of Clairvaux, *Sermons on the Song of Songs*, 8.
4 Augustine, *The City of God*, bk. XXII, ch. 30.
5 This chapter was written on the Feast of the Transfiguration.
6 Bernard of Clairvaux, *On Loving God*, ch. 5.
7 Frank Weston, Bishop of Zanzibar, 'Our Present Duty', Concluding Address, Anglo-Catholic Congress, 1923.
8 *Spiritual Exercises*, para. 23.
9 *Spiritual Exercises*, para. 179.
10 G. B. Timms, 'Word of the Father, source of all things living',
New English Hymnal 315.
11 Extract from 'Eurydice' from *Collected Poems by Edith Sitwell*
reprinted by permission of Peters Fraser & Dunlop (www.petersfraser
dunlop.com) on behalf of the Estate of Edith Sitwell.
12 Baptism Rite of the Church of England.
13 Ambrose of Milan, *On the Mysteries*.

The priesthood is the love of the heart of Jesus

✠

Ut in Omnibus Glorificetur Deus

Appendix 1

❧

PRAYER PRACTICE FOR SITTING IN THE COMPASSIONATE GAZE OF JESUS

We're often aware of the critical glare of others and can easily come to 'sit' in that place. So it's important that we practise sitting in the *compassionate* gaze of Jesus in order to undermine that tendency and focus our attention on God's love for us.

1 Choose a passage of Scripture that speaks of God's loving presence, e.g. the Woman at the Well (John 4.4–15); the Man born Blind (Matt. 20.29–34).

2 Decide how long you'll spend in prayer *(e.g. 15/20 mins)*.

   - Squat on a meditation stool or in a chair that will hold your back firmly but in a relaxed manner.
   - Allow your senses to be present to the place you have adopted.
   - For a few moments, breathe slowly – breathe in the love of God and breath out whatever you need to let go of.

3 Read the passage of Scripture, slowly, twice.

   - Notice what thoughts/ideas/concerns etc. come to your attention. Acknowledge them and try to place them behind you – let go of them whenever they begin to attract you again.

4 Now imagine the place where this compassionate encounter is to take place and pay attention to the scene. Notice
the scene through all your senses:

- Feel the hot sun beating down. Smell the dust. Feel the
clothing you're wearing, the sweat rolling down you. See
the look in the face of the woman or man and notice
what they say. Note the reaction of any others. Above
all, watch Jesus – the way he walks, his gestures, the
look in his eyes, the expression on his face. Hear him
speak the words that are recorded in the Gospel. Go on
to imagine other words he might have spoken or actions
he may have expressed.
- Then imagine Jesus approach you – with a kindly, compassionate expression. Let yourself become aware that
the concern he had for the person, he has for you. He
wants to heal you, forgive you – love you. He wants to
hold you in a compassionate embrace. *(If you find it
impossible to imagine the scene, then either recall times
when you have experienced compassion or sense someone holding you, lovingly. In a spirit of generosity, pray
as you're able; don't try to force it. Be sure that God
will speak to you, whether through your memory, understanding, intellect, emotions or imagination.)*
- Sense the loving kindness Jesus has for you. Allow yourself to be held in that compassionate gaze. Relish it. Let
it seep through your defences and notice any resistance
there may be.
- If you realize your attention is wandering,* bring it back
to this encounter.
- Pay attention to what arises in your prayer – reflect on it
and have a conversation with the Lord, don't let it just
rumble on. *(I still recall the powerful way I called out*

---

* When engaging with your thoughts return ever so gently to the
scene. Thoughts include body sensations, images, reflections, etc.

to Jesus when praying with the account of Peter sinking beneath the waves during the storm at sea and how I really became conscious of Jesus reaching out to me.)

- If you can, begin to tell Jesus what lies in your heart. Open it to him and express whatever you want to say. Listen to any sensed response.

5 As the period comes to an end, remain in silence with eyes closed for a couple of minutes quietly letting the experience settle into you. Finally, express your gratitude for the way you are held in God's compassionate gaze in words such as:

May the centre of my being be one with the
Heart of Christ. Amen.

(If appropriate, Ignatius encourages us to repeat these experiences to see if there's anything more to discover as we seek to be present to God's compassionate gaze.)

Appendix 2

৯৹

PRAYING OUR FAREWELLS

Before the Dismissal, a suitable hymn is sung. Then:

Priest: We are God's people gathered here;
All: **let us kneel before God's footstool.**
Priest: Let us pray:
Lord Jesus Christ,
we thank you that in this wonderful Sacrament
you have given us the memorial of your passion:
grant us so to reverence the sacred mysteries
of your Body and Blood
that we may know within ourselves
and show forth in our lives
the fruits of your redemption;
for you are alive and reign
with the Father and the Holy Spirit,
one God, now and forever. **Amen.**

The Priest hands the sacred vessels and chasuble to a Server and says:

And the Word became flesh and dwelt among us,
and we have seen his glory,
All: **the glory as of the Father's only Son,
full of grace and truth.**

Priest: God of all grace,
            your Son fed the hungry with the bread of his life
            and the word of his kingdom,
            renew your people with your heavenly grace,
            and in all our weakness,
            sustain us by your true and living bread;
            who is alive and reigns, now and forever. **Amen.**

*The Priest hands the Book of the Gospels to an appropriate
person and says:*

            Your word is a lantern to my feet,
All: **and a light upon my path.**
            Your words are spirit, Lord, and they are life;
All: **may they ever be on our lips and in our heart.**

The Churchwardens come forward and say:

            **The Lord shall watch over your going out and
            your coming in;**
Priest: From this time forth and forevermore.
Minister: Gracious God,
            your Spirit hovers over the Church
            to guide and sanctify it;
            hear our prayer which we offer for all your people,
            that, in their vocation and ministry,
            each may serve you in holiness and truth
            through Christ our Lord. **Amen.**

The Priest says to the Churchwardens:

            This is the House of God;
All: **and the Gate of Heaven.**
Priest: God of our pilgrimage,
            the desire of our hearts and longings,
            may this place always be a well of holiness
            and a sign to your presence in our midst.

Let all who seek you be welcome here
and find their home with all your saints
in Christ, our hidden companion on the Way.
Amen.

*S/He hands back the keys of the church to the Churchwardens
who say:*

May the Lord bless you
in your continuing priestly vocation. **Amen.**

Priest: As I leave, I give thanks
for all that you have given to me;
I assure you of my love and prayers.

All: **As you experience the pain of change,
and the insecurity of moving on,
we pray that you may also experience
the blessing of inner growth.**

Priest: I know that God goes with me.

Minister: Let us silently offer our prayers to God
and ask a blessing on ... (and ...)

*S/He kneels for the blessing of the Church. The Church-
wardens and others lay hands on him/her in a moment of
silent prayer after which they invite the congregation to stand
and extend their right hand as they join in the blessing:*

**To the prayers of our blessed Lady
we commend you.
May** (Parish patron), **pray for you.
May all the saints of God, pray for you.
May the holy angels befriend you
and watch around you to protect you.
May the Lord bless you and watch over you,
the Lord make his face shine upon you
and be gracious to you,
the Lord look kindly on you and give you peace.**

Priest: Thanks be to God.

The Churchwardens lead the Priest to the entrance as the final hymn is sung

Minister: The Mass is ended,
          go in peace to love and serve the Lord!
All: **Thanks be to God.**

© *John-Francis Friendship*

Appendix 3

ॐ

A FORM OF CONFESSION AND ABSOLUTION

The penitent says:
Bless me, Mother/Father, for I have sinned.

The priest says:
May the Lord be on your lips and in your heart
that you may truly and rightly confess your sins,
in the name of the Father ✠ and of the Son and of the
Holy Spirit. Amen.

The penitent says:
I confess to almighty God
and before the whole company of heaven,
that I have sinned through my own fault,
in my thoughts and in my words,
in what I have done and in what I have failed to do.
Especially *(since my last Confession)*
I accuse myself of the following sins:
Here the penitent confesses their sins.
For these and all the other sins that I cannot now remember
I am heartily sorry,
firmly mean to do better, most humbly ask pardon of God
and of you penance (advice) and absolution. Amen.
(The priest may respond with a few words and pronounce absolution.)

Our Lord Jesus Christ, who has left power to his Church
to absolve all who truly repent and believe in him,
of his great mercy forgive you your offences;
and by his authority committed to me,
I absolve you from all your sins, in the name of the Father,
and of the Son ✠ and of the Holy Spirit. Amen.

The Passion of our Lord Jesus Christ,
whatsoever good you have done or evil you endure,
be to you for the remission of sins, the increase of grace,
and the reward of eternal life:
And the blessing of God almighty,
Father, Son ✠ and Holy Spirit,
be with you now and always. Amen.

Go in peace; the Lord has put away your sins,
and pray for me, a sinner too. Amen.

Appendix 4

❧

A SIMPLE 'EXAMEN'

(from 'Sleeping with Bread' by Dennis, Sheila and Matt Linn)

Preparation

Do whatever helps you to experience God's unconditional love.

Put your feet on the floor. Breathe in that unconditional love and let your breath seep down through your body into your toes. When you breathe out, breathe out all that is preventing you knowing yourself as a loved child of God. Then:

1 Place your hand on your heart and ask God to bring to your heart the moment today for which you are *most grateful*. When were you most able to give and receive love today?

   Ask yourself what was said and done in the moment that made it so special. Breathe in the gratitude you feel and receive life again from that moment.

2 Ask God to bring to your heart the moment today for which you are least grateful. When were you least able to give and receive love?

Ask yourself what was said and done in that moment that made it so difficult. Be with whatever you feel without trying to change or fix it in any way. You may wish to take deep breaths and let God's love fill you just as you are.

3 Give thanks for what you have experienced.

Appendix 5

ॐ

LECTIO DIVINA

Lectio divina is an ancient way of contemplatively reading Scripture kept alive within the monastic tradition. By tradition, it follows four stages:

Lectio: reverential reading of a portion of text, usually Scripture
Meditatio: *meditation*
Oratio: *prayer*
Contemplatio: *resting in God's embrace*

Lectio
First Reading
Read the passage aloud and listen for a word, phrase or idea that *captures your attention*. As you recognize a word, phrase or idea, *focus your attention on that word, repeating it.* Silence.

Second Reading
Read text again and focus your attention on *how the word, phrase or idea speaks to your life*. Silence.

Meditatio
What does it mean for you? How is Christ speaking to you through this word, phrase or idea? 'Chew' on it so that you take from it what God wants to give.

Oratio

Reflecting on the Word of God, leave thinking aside and simply let your heart speak to God.

Contemplatio

Let go of all this and simply rest in the Word of God. Listen at the deepest level of your being to God who speaks within you with a still small voice.

Appendix 6

❧

VESTING PRAYERS

Washing hands
Give strength to my hands, Lord, to wipe away every stain, that I may be able to serve you in purity of mind and body.

Amice
Lord, set on my head the helmet of salvation that I may overcome the assaults of the devil.

Alb
Make me white, O Lord, and cleanse my heart; that being made white in the blood of the Lamb I may have the fruition of everlasting life.

Girdle
Gird me, O Lord, with the cincture of purity, and quench in my heart the fire of lust, that the virtue of continence and chastity may abide in me.

Maniple
May I deserve, O Lord, to bear the maniple of weeping and sorrow in order that I may joyfully reap the reward of my labours.

Stole

Restore to me, Lord, the stole of immortality which I lost through the transgression of our first parents and, unworthy as I am to approach these sacred mysteries, may I yet gain eternal joy.

Dalmatic (deacon and bishop)

Lord, endow me with the garment of salvation, the vestment of joy, and with the dalmatic of justice ever encompass me.

Chasuble

O Lord, who has said, 'My yoke is easy and my burden is light,' grant that I may so carry it as to merit grace. Amen.

✠

Bibliography

❧

The priesthood

Cowley, I., *The Contemplative Minister: Learning to lead from the still centre*, The Bible Reading Fellowship, 2015.

Marmion, Blessed Columba, *Christ, the Ideal of the Priest*, Ignatius Press, 2005.

Oldknow, J. and Crake, A. D. (compiled and arranged by), *The Priest's Book of Private Devotions*, Mowbray, 1933.

Pritchard, J., *The Life and Work of a Priest*, SPCK, 2007.

Ramsey, M., *The Christian Priest Today*, SPCK, 2009.

Robinson, H. M., *The Cardinal*, (a novel), 1950 (reprint edition: The Overlook Press, 2013).

Sansom, J. (ed.), *The Works of the Right Reverend Father in God John Cosin, Lord Bishop of Durham*, Library of Anglo-Catholic Theology, John Henry Parker, 1843–55.

Smolarski, D. C., *How Not to Say Mass*, Paulist Press, 2013.

Walker, Revd A. S., 'The Usage, Understanding and Theology of the Daily Office Amongst Anglican Clergy Today', PhD thesis in Theology and Mission, King's College, London, 2015 (extracts used with permission).

Spiritual direction

Barry, W. A., and Connelly, W. J., *The Practice of Spiritual Direction*, 2nd edition, Bravo Ltd, 2009.

Nouwen, H., *Spiritual Direction: Wisdom for the Long Walk of Faith*, SPCK, 2011.

Spirituality – classics

Brother Lawrence, *The Practice of the Presence of God*, Dover Publications, 2005.

The Cloud of Unknowing (latter half of the fourteenth century; author unknown), Penguin Classics, 2001.

de Caussade, J.-P., *Self-Abandonment to Divine Providence*, TAN Books, 1987.

Fleming SJ., D. L., *A Contemporary Reading of the Spiritual Exercises*, The Institute of Jesuit Sources, 1980.

Julian of Norwich, *Revelations of Divine Love*, translated by T. Wolter, Penguin Classics, 1973.

The Life and Doctrine of Saint Catherine of Genoa. Compiled by her Confessor, Don Cattaneo Marabotto, Christian Classics Ethereal Library, 2009.

Puhl SJ, L. J., *The Spiritual Exercises of St. Ignatius*, Loyola Press, 1951.

The Spiritual Doctrine of St. Catherine of Genoa, TAN Books, 1989.

St John of the Cross, 'Sayings of Light and Love' (a collection of aphorisms as a starting point for prayer and reflection), from *The Collected Works of St. John of the Cross*, translated by Kieran Kavanaugh, OCD and Otilio Rodriguez, OCD, revised edition, ICS Publications, 1991.

Spirituality – contemporary

Alphonso SJ, H., *Discovering Your Personal Vocation: The Search for Meaning through the Spiritual Exercises*, Paulist Press, 2001.

Bonhoeffer, D., *Psalms: The Prayer Book of the Bible*, translated by Sr. Isabel Mary SLG, Fairacres Publications, 1982.

de Chardin SJ, T., *The Hymn of the Universe*, Harper Perennial, 1969.

Hughes SJ, G., *In Search of a Way*, DLT, 1980.

Laird OSB, M., *Into the Silent Land – The Practice of Contemplation*, DLT, 2006.

Linn, D., S. and M., *Sleeping with Bread: Holding What Gives You Life*, Paulist Press, 1995.

Lonsdale SJ, D., *Eyes to See, Ears to Hear: An Introduction to Ignatian Spirituality*, Orbis Books, 2000.

Martin SJ, M., *The Jesuit Guide to (Almost) Everything*, Harper One, 2010.

Quoist, M., *Prayers of Life*, Gill and MacMillan, 1965.

Traub SJ, G. (ed.), *An Ignatian Spirituality Reader*, Loyola Press, 2008.

van Breemen SJ, P. G., *As Bread That Is Broken*, Dimension Books, 1974.

Vanstone, W. H., *The Stature of Waiting*, DLT, 1982.

Religious life

Anglican Religious Life Yearbook, Canterbury Press.

Bodo, M., *The Way of St. Francis: The Challenge of Franciscan Spirituality for Everyone*, St Anthony Messenger Press, 1995.

First Rule of St. Francis (1221) There are many excellent books on Franciscan spirituality, one of the best being by Br. Ramon SSF: *Franciscan Spirituality: Following St Francis Today*, SPCK, 2008.

The Little Flowers of St. Francis, Dover Publications, 2003.

Principles of the Society of St Francis, in *Daily Office SSF*, Mowbray, 1992 *(extracts used with permission)*

de Waal, E., *Seeking God: The Way of St. Benedict*, Liturgical Press, 2001.

Other

Loades, A. and MacSwain, R. (eds), *The Truth-Seeking Heart: Austen Farrar and His Writings*, Canterbury Press, 2006.

Schillebeeckx, E., *Christ the Sacrament of the Encounter with God*, Sheed & Ward, 1963.

The Spiritual Association of the Compassionate Hearts of Jesus and Mary. An online, ecumenical association offering resources for the 'conversion of the heart' (http://cchjm.org/).

Further notes

Those Anglicans who feel called to celibacy might find help by contacting the *Single Consecrated Life*, a 'Fresh Expression' of monasticism within the Church of England (http://www.singleconsecratedlife-anglican.org.uk/). Roman Catholics should contact the *National Office for Vocation* for advice (http://www.ukvocation.org/).

SLG Press produce excellent, reasonably priced pamphlets and booklets on a variety of aspects of Christian spirituality. Grove Booklets also publish a series on spirituality; recent topics have included pilgrimage, silence, mindfulness and the Jesus Prayer.